On
Socialism
In One Country

Selected Writings from
Lenin
Conclusion from Stalin

Selected writings from Lenin & Stalin researched and
compiled for various articles on the subject.

Erdogan A

No Copy Rights

Table of Contents

Introduction
Trotsky, An answer to Stalinist Critics   14

Trotsky, Forming The Government   24

Lenin, On the Slogan for a US of Europe 42

Engels to Kautsky   48

Lenin, The Military Programme of the Proletarian Revolution
                                      50
Lenin, The "Disarmament" Slogan   55

Lenin, Report on the Activities of Th CPC 58

Lenin, Report on Foreign Policy   84

Lenin, State and revolution   109

Lenin, First All-Russia Congress on Adult Education   120

The Achievements and Difficulties of the Soviet Government 140

Lenin, Speech At A Plenary Session Of The Moscow Soviet 187

Stalin, On the Final Victory of Socialism in the U.S.S.R. 197

Introduction

Internet is full of - actually over 8 million - writings about" Socialism **in one country "being a theory put forth by Joseph Stalin, "** being a **betrayal of Leninist theory"** etc. This is not a coincidence but an inevitable result of ideological struggle between the bourgeoisie, their servile petty bourgeois and Marxism Leninism as the ideology of laboring masses. **It is one of the cheap falsification of history, distortion of facts,** simply: cheap propaganda directed at average people and petty bourgeois intellectuals in return which makes it possible for **the petty bourgeois** and the reaction **to hide behind "leftist" mask** and gives them the opportunity to **attack Socialist theories as "critics from the left"** without appearing as reactionary.

Their master Trotsky who supplied a vast material to imperialists and anti-communists to fight against communism, also supplied the tactics for it. According to Trotsky, the pioneer of this lie:

"Lenin was only referring to the establishment of a **'proletarian dictatorship' in a single country"**. *Trotsky, The Third International*

And same Trotsky said:

Lenin said ; "For the success of socialism in Russia a certain period of time of at least a few months is necessary."
""**I remember very well** how during the first period, in the Smolny, **Lenin repeated time and time again** in the Council of People's Commissars: half a year from now **we'll have socialism** and we'll be the most powerful state on earth... **He believed what he said.** " *Trotsky, On Lenin*

According to Trotsky Lenin believed in "Socialism in One country" then it was not a "betrayal to Leninism" on Stalin's part, but it was the continuation of Lenin's believe, and Stalin interpreted Lenin's views correctly.

3

Let's go back to history of the theory where "Socialism in one country" has become the theory and practical solution for an isolated revolutionary state.

Lenin's theory of "socialism in one country" goes back to 1915 where even contrary to the distorted view, Lenin was not **"merely referring to socialist revolution in one country,"** * but also contrary to views of scholars such as Carr, Lenin was referring to the **possibility of constructing a socialist economy in a single country.** *Carr, A History, and some others,*

Lenin, in his article `on the slogan for a US of Europe, **clearly states his view** which is ignored stubbornly in all discussions. Lenin says:

"After expropriating the capitalists and organizing **their own socialist production,** the victorious proletariat of that country will arise against the rest of the world — the capitalist world — attracting to its cause the oppressed classes of other countries, stirring uprisings in those countries against the capitalists, and in case of need using even armed force **against the exploiting classes and their states.**" *Lenin, On the Slogan for a US of Europe*

Lenin was clearly stating that for an isolated revolutionary state, it would be feasible to build a socialist economy.

Lenin's referenced article debating the slogan, published at Sotsial-Demokrat No. 44, August 23, 1915. Lenin was stating that:

"It might lead to an incorrect interpretation concerning the impossibility of the victory of socialism in one country and concerning the relationship of such a country with the others. **The unevenness of economic and political development** is an unconditional law of capitalism. It follows from this that the victory of socialism initially in several or even in one, separately taken capitalist country is possible. **Having expropriated the capitalists and having organised socialist production at home,** the victorious proletariat of this country would rise against the remaining capitalist world... in case of need even coming out with military force against the exploiting classes and their states... **The free unification of nations in socialism is impossible without a more or less prolonged, stubborn struggle of socialist republics against the backward states.** " Lenin, "'On the slogan of the United States of Europe

Through this article Lenin was suggesting that before engaging in revolutionary world war, the victorious proletariat, the **proletarian dictatorship** would have to **build a socialist economy at home.** This suggestion of Lenin clearly derives from the **belief that the victory of socialism in one country is possible.**

Regarding the same issue, Engels was telling to Kautsky in his 12 September 1882 dated letter:

"One thing alone is certain: **the victorious proletariat** can force no blessings of any kind upon **any foreign nation** without **undermining its own victory** by so doing. Which of course **by no means excludes defensive wars of various kinds.** "

Lenin in his article dated September 1916'The Military Programme of the Proletarian Revolution referring to Engels was stating :

""**the victory of socialism in one country** does not at one stroke eliminate all wars in general. On the contrary, it presupposes wars. The development of capitalism proceeds extremely unevenly in different countries. It cannot be otherwise under commodity production. From this it follows irrefutably that **socialism cannot achieve victory simultaneously in all countries.** It will **achieve victory first in one or several countries,** while the others will for some time remain bourgeois or pre-bourgeois. This is bound to create not only friction, but a direct attempt on the part of the bourgeoisie of other countries to crush **the socialist state's victorious proletariat.** In such cases, a war on our part would be a legitimate and just war. It would be a war for socialism, for the liberation of other nations from the bourgeoisie. **Engels was perfectly right when,** in his letter to Kautsky of September 12, 1882, he clearly stated that it was possible for already victorious socialism to wage "defensive wars". **What he had in mind** was defense of the **victorious proletariat against the bourgeoisie of other countries.** " *'The Military Programme of the Proletarian Revolution*

He continued saying:

'**Only after we will have overthrown,** finally vanquished and expropriated the bourgeoisie in the whole world, and not only in one country, **wars will become impossible.**' *The Military Programme of the Proletarian Revolution*

On another article dated October 1916 Lenin says:

"Wars are possible between **one country in which socialism has been victorious** and other, bourgeois or reactionary, countries.'" The "Disarmament" Slogan

In July 1916, Lenin said:

"An **economic revolution will be a stimulus** to all peoples to strive for socialism; but at the same time *(counter)* revolutions—**against the socialist state**—and wars are possible." *Lenin, The Discussion On Self-Determination Summed Up*

As it is indisputably shown from the above quotations, the concept of "**socialism in one country**" **is not** a theory put forward by Stalin, **but it is a Leninist theory.**

It is the falsification and cheap propaganda of **permanent-counter revolutionaries** who choose to **wait indefinitely** for an "**international revolution**" to come, yet at the same time attack those who fight for revolution.

In 1918 Lenin was mentioning this type of bourgeois servile:

"…when we are told that **the victory of socialism is possible only on a world scale**, we regard this merely as an attempt, a particularly **hopeless attempt,** on the part of the **bourgeoisie and its voluntary and involuntary supporters** to distort the irrefutable truth." *Lenin, "Speech to the Third All-Russia Congress of Soviets"*

And same year He mentions the permanent- revolution-wait-ers:

"**I know that there are**, of course, sages who think they are very clever and **even call themselves Socialists**, who assert that power should not have been seized **until the revolution had broken out in all countries**. They do not suspect that by speaking in this way **they are deserting the revolution** and **going over to the side of the bourgeoisie.** To **wait until** the toiling classes, bring about a **revolution on an international scale** means that everybody should stand stock-still in expectation. **That is nonsense."** *Lenin, "Speech delivered at a joint meeting of the All-Russian Central Executive Committee and the Moscow Soviet*

As the facts come out and their lies are confronted, **they choose new tactics,** new lies and **they create new confusions.** They extract quotes for the "impossibility of socialism in one country by **confusing socialism- first phase,** and **communism - second phase,** to one of which Lenin responds:

""when a learned professor, followed by the philistine…, talks of wild utopias, of the demagogic promises of the Bolsheviks, of **the impossibility of "introducing" socialism, it is the higher stage,** or phase, **of communism he has in mind,** which no one has ever promised or even thought to "introduce", because, **generally speaking, it cannot be "introduced".**

What is usually called **socialism was termed by Marx the "first", or lower, phase** of communist society. Insofar as the means of production becomes common property, the word "communism" is also applicable here, **providing** we **do not forget** that **this is not complete communism."** -higher stage. *Lenin State and revolution*

7

Lenin in his speech was confirming both what socialism is and the existence of socialism in Russia, in one country.

"Socialism is the first stage of communism: but it is not worthwhile arguing about words.....We must save the workers even if they are unable to work. If we keep them alive for the next few years, we shall save the country, **save society and socialism."** *Lenin, First All-Russia Congress on Adult Education*

January 1918, at the Third All-Union Congress of Soviets, Lenin said that the **Soviet republic is a socialist republic:**

"**We never had any illusions on that score,** and we know how difficult is the road that leads from capitalism to socialism. But it is our duty to say that **our Soviet Republic is a socialist republic** because we have taken this road, and **our words will not be empty words."** *Lenin, Third All-Russia Congress Of Soviets Of Workers', Soldiers' And Peasants' Deputies*

And a year later in 1919 repeats that:
"**We have achieved this objective in one country,** and this confronts us with a second task. Since Soviet power has been established, **since the bourgeoisie has been overthrown in one country**, the second task is to wage the struggle on a world scale, on a different plane, **the struggle of the proletarian state surrounded by capitalist states."** *Lenin, "The Achievements and Difficulties of the Soviet Government"*

In 1922 Lenin says:

"**Socialism is no longer a matter of the distant future,** or an abstract picture, or an icon. We still retain our old bad opinion of icons. **We have dragged socialism into everyday life,** and here we must find our way. " *Lenin, Speech At A Plenary Session Of The Moscow Soviet*

In 1923 Lenin responses to the critiques:

You say that civilization is necessary for the building of socialism. Very good. But why could we not first create such prerequisites of civilization in our country by the expulsion of the landowners and the Russian capitalists, and then start moving toward socialism? **Where, in what books, have you read that such variations of the customary historical sequence of events are impermissible or impossible**?" *Lenin, "Our Revolution"*

" **Socialism in one country** " has been Lenin's thinking since 1915.

As the truth comes out, some bourgeois revisionists **accept the fact that it was Lenin's theory** and adapt themselves to, and **come up with new claims**, one of which is that L**enin's views lack the coherence, that he contradicts himself** by rejecting in one writing and then accepting in another. Aside from being a blatant ignorant of Marxist Dialectics on their part, the claim is **related to their tactics in confusing** the scientific meaning of socialism and communism where they take the "terms" used by Lenin or Stalin **out of context** and without any regard **to the "two phase of transition"** - Lower and higher phase.

Lenin clearly explains the reason of the **use of term** " **Communism**":

"**Insofar as** the means of production become common property," Lenin says, "**the word 'communism' is also applicable here,**" but Lenin warns: " **provided** we do **not forget that this is not complete communism.**" *Lenin, State and Revolution, Presentation of the Question by Marx*

Another related lie is presented in various forms - of **Lenin's belief** that there is no possibility of long-term peaceful coexistence between the single socialist state and the capitalist world, but "**Stalin believed** that the isolated socialist state could in principle coexist **indefinitely** with the capitalist states."

Since they never read Stalin, they discourage people to read Stalin and encourage them to believe in their lies, we should note what Stalin said on the subject with the quote from Lenin:

This is what Lenin says on this score:

"**We are living not merely in a State but in a system of States,** and it is inconceivable that the Soviet Republic should continue to coexist for a long period side by side with imperialist States. Ultimately one or other must conquer. Meanwhile, a number of terrible clashes between the Soviet Republic and the bourgeois States is inevitable. This means that if the proletariat, as the ruling class, wants to and will rule, it must prove this also by military organization." (Collected Works, Vol. 24. P. 122.)

And further:

"**We are surrounded by people, classes and governments which openly express their hatred for us.** We must remember that we are at all times but a hair's breadth from invasion." (Collected Works, Vol. 27. P. 117.)

Indeed, **it would be ridiculous and stupid** to close our eyes to the **capitalist encirclement** and to think that our external enemies, the fascists, for example, will not, if the opportunity arises, make an attempt at a military attack upon the U.S.S.R. **Only blind braggarts** or **masked enemies** who desire to lull the vigilance of our people **can think like that.**

No less ridiculous would it be to deny that in the event of the slightest success of military intervention, the interventionists would try to **destroy the Soviet system in the districts they occupied and restore the bourgeois system.** `` *Stalin, On the Final Victory of Socialism in the U.S.S.R.*

Struggle against capitalism at the same time is an ideological struggle. That is why, it is expected that those who owns the means of production, owning at the same time the means of mental production will do anything in their power, use every means and methods in this ideological war. They will bury the facts under millions of garbage in internet , on the shelves of libraries, they will prepare a list of `reactionary` data disguised in left phrases for the university students for their thesis in related subject, they will pay and award those academicians who can "**rewrite the history**" **and** "**falsify, revise** " the theories serving best to their interests. The truth is stubborn. Stalin had said:

"I know that after my death a pile of rubbish will be heaped on my grave, but the wind of History will sooner or later sweep it away without mercy." *Quoted in Felix Chuev, Molotov Remembers*

E.A

April 2020

Trotsky's falsification and confusion between the "victory of Socialist Revolution" in any given country, and the "Complete victory of socialist revolution" in a world scale. Between the Defeat of capitalism in any given country -socialism, and the defeat of capitalism in world scale- communism.

Lenin on Socialism in One Country

Leon TrotskyAn Answer to Stalinist Critics– II, (November 1926)

Another passage from my works has been brought up against me – and here I come to the question of the possibility of the victory of socialism in one country – which reads as follows:

The contradictions in the position of the workers' government in a backward country with an overwhelming agrarian population can only be solved on an international scale and in the arena of the proletarian world revolution.

This was said in 1922. The accusing resolution makes the following statement:

The conference places on record that such views as these on the part of Comrade Trotsky and his followers, in the fundamental question of the character and prospects of our revolution, have nothing in common with the views of our party, with Leninism."

If it had been stated that a shade of difference existed – I do not find this even today – or that these views have not yet been precisely formulated (and I do not see the precise formulation). But it is stated quite flatly: these views "have nothing in common with the views of the party, with Leninism."

Here I must quote a few lines closely related to Leninism:

The **complete victory** of the socialist revolution in one country is unthinkable and demands the active co-operation of at least some advanced countries, among which we cannot count Russia.

It was not I who said this, but one greater than I. Lenin said this November 8, 1918. Not before the October Revolution, but on November 8, 1918, one year after we had seized power. If he had said nothing else but this, we could easily infer what we liked from it by tearing one sentence or the other out of its context. (A voice: "He was speaking of the final victory!") No, pardon me, he said: "demands the active cooperation." Here it is impossible to sidetrack from the main question to the question of "intervention," for it is plainly stated that the victory of socialism demands – not merely protection against intervention – but the cooperation of "at least some advanced countries, among which we cannot count Russia." (Voices: "And what follows from that?") This is not the only passage in which we see that not merely an intervention is meant. And thus the conclusion to be drawn is the fact that the standpoint which I have defended, to the effect that the internal contradictions arising out of the backwardness of our country must be solved by international revolution, is not my exclusive property, but that Lenin defended these same views, only incomparably more definitely and categorically.

We are told that this applied to the epoch in which the law of the unequal development of the capitalist countries is supposed to have been still unknown, that is, the epoch before imperialism. I cannot go thoroughly into this. But I must unfortunately place on record that Comrade Stalin commits a great theoretical and historical error here. The law of the unequal development of capitalism is older than imperialism. Capitalism is developing very unequally today in the various countries. But in the nineteenth century this inequality was greater than in the twentieth. At that time England was lord of the world, while Japan on the other hand was a feudal state closely confined within its own limits. At the time when serfdom was abolished among us, Japan began to adapt itself to capitalist civilization. China was, however, still wrapped in

13

the deepest slumber. And so forth. At this time the inequality of capitalist development was greater than now. Those inequalities were as well known to Marx and Engels as they are to us. Imperialism has developed a more "leveling tendency than has pre-imperialist capitalism, for the reason that financial capital is the most elastic form of capital. It is, however, indisputable that today, too, there are great inequalities in development. But if it is maintained that in the nineteenth century, before imperialism, capitalism developed less unequally, and the theory of the possibility of socialism in one country was therefore wrong at that time, whilst today, now that imperialism has increased the heterogeneity of development, the theory of socialism in one country has become correct, then this assertion contradicts all historical experience, and completely reverses fact. No, this will not do; other and more serious arguments must be sought: Comrade Stalin has written:

Those who deny the possibility of the establishment of socialism in one country must deny at the same time the justifiability of the October Revolution. (Stalin, Problems of Leninism, p. 215)

But in 1918 we heard from Lenin that the establishment of socialism requires the direct cooperation of some advanced countries, "among which we cannot count Russia." Yet Lenin did not deny the justifiability of the October Revolution. And he wrote as follows regarding this in 1918:

I know that there are some ingenious people (this was written against the adherents of Kautsky and Suchanov), who think themselves very clever, and even call themselves socialists; these maintain that we should not have seized power until revolution had broken out in all countries. They are not aware that in speaking thus they are deviating from revolution and going over to the bourgeoisie. To wait until the working masses, accomplish the international revolution is to wait till we are stiff and rigid, to wait till we are frozen to death. This is nonsense ...

I am sorry, but it goes on as follows:

This is nonsense. The difficulty of revolution is known to all of us. For the final victory can only be on an international scale and can only be brought about by the joint exertions of the workers of all countries. (Lenin, Vol. 15, page 287, written on May 14, 1918.)

Despite this, Lenin did not deny the "justifiability" of the October Revolution.

And further. In 1921 – not in 1914, but in 1921 – Lenin wrote:

In the advanced capitalist countries, there is a class of agricultural laborers, created by decades of wage work. It is only in countries where this class is sufficiently developed that the transition from capitalism to socialism is possible.

Here it is not a question of intervention but of the level of economic development and of the development of the class relations of the country.

In many of our works, and in all of our utterances in the press, we have emphasized that this is not the case in Russia, that in Russia the industrial workers are in the minority, and that the overwhelming majority are small farmers. Social revolution in such a country as this can only be finally successful under two conditions: firstly, the condition that it is supported at the right time by the social revolution in one or several more advanced countries ...

The other condition is the understanding between the proletariat and the majority of the peasant population ...

We know that only an understanding with the peasantry can save the socialist revolution in Russia, so long as social revolution has not broken out in other countries. This must be stated openly at all meetings, and in the whole press. (Lenin, speech at the Xth Party Congress of the RCP, 1921)

Lenin did not state that the understanding with the peasantry sufficed, enabling us to build up socialism independent of the fate of the international proletariat. No, this understanding is only one of the conditions. The other condition is the support to be given the revolution by other countries. He combines these two conditions with each other, emphasizing their special necessity for us as we live in a backward country.

And finally, it is brought up against me that I have stated that "a real advance of socialist economy in Russia is only possible after the victory of the proletariat in the most important countries of Europe." It is probable, comrades, that we have become inaccurate in the use of various terms. What do we understand under "socialist economy" in the strict sense of the term? We have great successes to record and are naturally proud of these. I have endeavored to describe them in my booklet, Toward Socialism or Capitalism, for the benefit of extent of these successes. Comrade Rykov's theses state that we are approaching the pre-war level. But this is not quite accurate. Is our population the same as before the war? No, it is larger. And the average consumption of industrial goods per head is considerably less than in 1913. The people's Supreme Economic Council calculates that in this respect we shall not regain the pre-war level until 1930. And then, what was the level of 1913? It was the level of misery, of backwardness, of barbarism. If we speak of socialist economy, and of a real advance in socialist economy, we mean: no antagonism between town and country, general content, prosperity, culture. This is what we understand under the real advance of socialist economy. And we are still far indeed from this goal. We have destitute children, we have unemployed, from the villages there come three million superfluous workers every year, half a million of whom seek work in the cities, where the industries cannot absorb more than 1,100,000 yearly. We have a right to be proud of what we have achieved, but we must not distort the historical perspective. What we have accomplished is not yet a real advance of socialist economy, but only the first serious steps on that long bridge leading from capitalism to socialism. Is this the same thing? By no means. The passage quoted against me stated the truth.

In 1922 Lenin wrote:

"But we have not yet even completed the foundation of our socialist economy, and the hostile forces of expiring capitalism may even yet deprive us of it again This must be clearly recognized and openly admitted, for there is nothing so dangerous as illusions and dizziness, especially at great heights. And there is nothing "frightful," nothing which can give the slightest cause for despair, in the recognition of this bitter truth, for we have always proclaimed and repeated that elementary truth of Marxism, that the joint efforts of the workers of some advanced countries are necessary for the victory of socialism." (Lenin, Complete Works, Russian edition, Vol. XX/2, page 487.)

The question here is therefore not of intervention, but of the joint efforts of several advanced countries for the establishment of socialism. Or was this written by Lenin before the epoch of imperialism, before the law of unequal development was known? No, he wrote this in 1922.

There is, however, another passage, in the article on cooperatives, one single passage, which is set up against everything else that Lenin wrote, or rather the attempt is made so to oppose it. (A voice: "Accidentally!") Not by any means accidentally. I am in full agreement with the sentence. It must be understood properly. The passage is as follows:

As a matter of fact, all the great means of production are in the possession of the state, the state power is in the hands of the proletariat: the alliance of this proletariat with the many millions of poor and poorest peasantry, the security of the leadership of this proletariat over the peasantry, etc.; is then this not everything which we require to enable us to build up out of the cooperatives, of the cooperatives alone, which we treated at one time in a step-motherly manner, as petty tradesman affairs and which we are now justified to a certain extent in so treating under the NEP – to build up out of the cooperatives alone the complete socialist state of society? This is not yet the establishment of the socialist state of society, but it is everything which is necessary and sufficient for this realization ...

(A voice: "You read much too quickly." Laughter) Then you must give me a few minutes more, comrades. (Laughter. A voice: "Right!") Right? I am agreed. (A voice: "That is just what we want.")

What is the question here? What elements are here enumerated? In the first place, the possession of the means of production; in the second, the power of the proletariat; thirdly, the alliance between the proletariat and the peasantry; fourthly, the proletarian leadership of the peasantry, and fifthly, the cooperatives. I ask you: does any one of you believe that socialism can be established in one single isolated country? Could perchance the proletariat in Bulgaria alone, if it had the peasantry behind it, seize power, build up the cooperatives and establish socialism? No, that would be impossible. Consequently, further elements are required in addition to the above: the geographical situation, natural wealth, techniques culture. Lenin enumerates here the conditions of the state power, property relations and the organizatory forms of the cooperatives. Nothing more. And he says that we, in order to establish socialism, need not proletarianize the peasantry, nor need we any fresh revolutions, but that we are able, with power in our hands, in alliance with the peasantry, and with the aid of the cooperatives, to carry our task to completion through the agency of these state and social forms and methods.

But, comrades, we know another definition which Lenin gave of socialism. According to this definition, socialism is equal to soviet power plus electrification. Is electrification cancelled in the passage just quoted? No, it is not cancelled. Everything which Lenin otherwise said about the establishment of socialism – and I have adduced clear formulations above – is supplemented by this quotation, but not cancelled. For electrification is not something to be carried out in a vacuum, but under certain conditions, under the conditions imposed by the world market and the world economy, which are very tangible facts. The world economy is not mere theoretical generalization, but a definite and powerful reality, whose laws encompass us; a fact of which every year of our development convinces us.

Leon Trotsky
An Answer to Stalinist Critics – II
(November 1926)
International Press Correspondence, 1927

Forming the Government

Leon Trotsky

Lenin (1925)

THE power in Petersburg was won. There it was a question of forming the government.

"What name shall we use?" Lenin considered aloud. "Not minister, that is a repulsive, worn-out designation."

"We might say commissars," I suggested, "but there are too many commissars now. Perhaps chief commissar ... No, 'chief' sounds bad. What about people's commissars?"

"People's Commissars? As for me, I like it. And the government as a whole?"

"Council of People's Commissars?6#8221;

"Council of People's Commissars," Lenin repeated. "That is splendid. That smells of revolution."

I remember this last expression literally.

Behind the scenes tedious discussions went on with Wikshel, the Left Social Revolutionaries, and others. I can give little information on this subject. I only remember Lenin's furious indignation at Wikshel's shameless demands, and his no less furious indignation at those among us who were impressed by these demands. But we continued the discussions for, as things stood, we had to reckon with Wikshel.

At Comrade Kamenief's initiative the law introduced by Kerensky about the death penalty for soldiers was repealed. I no longer remember exactly where Kamenief made this motion; but probably in the Revolutionary Military Committee and apparently on the very morning of the 25th of October. I remember that it occurred in my presence and that I made no objections. Lenin was not yet there. It was evidently before his arrival in Smolny. When he learned of this first legislative act his anger knew no bounds.

"That is madness," he repeated. "How can we accomplish a revolution without shooting? Do you think you can settle with your enemies if you disarm? What repressive measures have you then? Imprisonment? Who pays any attention to that in a time of bourgeois war when every party hopes for victory?"

Kamenief tried to show that it was only a question of the repeal of the death penalty that Kerensky had introduced especially for deserting soldiers. But Lenin was not to be appeased. It was clear to him that this decree did not mean a cessation of the unheard of difficulties that we faced.

"It is a mistake," he repeated, "an inadmissible weakness. Pacifist illusion ..." He proposed changing the decree at once. We told him this would make an extraordinarily unfavorable impression. Finally someone said: "the best thing is to resort to shooting only when there is no other way." And it was left at that.

The bourgeois Social Revolutionary Menshevist press, from the first days after the revolution, formed a unanimous chorus of wolves, jackals, and mad dogs. The Novoe Vremya tried to strike a "loyal" tone and dropped its tail between its legs.

"Shall we not tame this pack?" Vladimir Ilyich asked at every opportunity. "For God's sake, what kind of dictatorship is that!"

The newspapers had taken up especially the words "steal the stolen" and distorted it in all ways, in proverbs, poems and feuilletons.

"And now they won't let go of this 'steal the stolen'," Lenin once said in comic despair.

"From whom did these words come?" I asked. "Or are they invented?"

"No, I once actually said them," Lenin answered. "I said it and forgot it, and they have made a whole program out of it." And he made a joking gesture.

Everyone who knows anything about Lenin knows very well that one of his strongest sides was the ability to separate the essence of a thing from its form. But this does not contradict in any way the fact that he valued the form also extraordinarily, for he knew the power of the formal on the mind, and thereby changed the formal into the material. From the moment that the Provisional Government was overthrown Lenin officiated as the government in large things as well as small. – We had as yet no apparatus; connection with the country was lacking; the employees were on strike; Wikshel cut the telephone connection with Moscow; we had neither money nor an army. But Lenin took hold of absolutely everything by means of statutes, decrees, and commands in the name of the government. Naturally he was further removed than any one from a superstitious adherence to formal oaths. He had recognized too clearly that our power lay in the new state apparatus, which was built up by the masses, by the Petrograd districts. But to combine the work coming from above, from the abandoned or wrecked government offices, with the productive work from below, this tone of formal energy was necessary, the tone of a government that to-day is a mere idea, but to-morrow or the day after will be the power and consequently must act to-day as the power. This formalism was also necessary to discipline our own brotherhood. Over the stormy element, over the revolutionary improvisations of the foremost proletarian groups, were gradually spun the threads of a government apparatus.

Lenin's office and mine in Smolny were in opposite ends of the building. The corridor that connected us, or rather separated us, was so long that Vladimir Ilyich laughingly suggested establishing a bicycle connection. We were connected by telephone and sailors were constantly running in bringing important notices from Lenin. On little slips of paper were two or three expressive sentences, each categorically formulated, the most important words two or three times underlined, and at the end a question that was also direct to the point. Several times a day I went through the endless corridor, that resembled a bee-hive, to Vladimir Ilyich's room. Military questions were the center of the conversations. The work for the Foreign Ministry I had left entirely to Comrades Markin and Salkind. I confined myself to drawing up a few agitatory notes and to seeing a few people.

The German attack presented the most difficult problems, which we had no means of solving, and also not the slightest idea how we should find these means, nor how we should create them. The draft written by me: The socialist fatherland is in danger, was discussed with the Left Social Revolutionaries. As recruits of internationalism the title of the appeal alarmed the latter. On the other hand, Lenin thoroughly approved of it. "That shows at once the change, from our cessation to the defense of the fatherland, at 180 degrees. It is exactly what we need!" In one of the last points of the draft there was the question of the immediate execution of anyone who gave assistance to the enemy. The Left Social Revolutionary Steinberg, whom a curious wind had driven into the revolution and even into the Council of People's Commissars, raised objections to this severe threat as it destroyed the "pathos of the appeal."

"On the contrary," exclaimed Lenin, "just there lies the real revolutionary pathós (he displaced the accent ironically). Do you think we can be victors without the most severe revolutionary terror?"

That was the period when Lenin, at every passing opportunity, emphasized the absolute necessity of the terror. All signs of sentimentality, laziness, or indifference – and all these were present even though in an attenuated form – did not enrage him in and for themselves, but as a sign that even the heads of the workmen's class did not yet sufficiently estimate the unheard – of difficulties of the problems, which could only be solved by measures of equally unheard – of energy.

"They," said Lenin speaking of the enemy, "are faced by the danger of losing everything. And moreover they have hundreds of thousands of men who have gone through the school of war, sated, determined, officers ready for anything, ensigns, bourgeois, and heirs of landowners, police, and well-to-do peasants. And there are, pardon the expression, 'revolutionaries' who imagine we should complete the revolution in love and kindness. Yes? Where did they go to school? What do they understand by dictatorship? What will become of a dictatorship if one is a weakling?"

We heard such tirades from him a dozen times a day and they were always aimed at someone among those present who was suspected of "pacifism." Lenin let no opportunity pass, when they spoke in his presence of the revolution and the dictatorship, particularly if this happened at the meetings of the Council of People's Commissars, or in the presence of the Left Social Revolutionaries or hesitating Communists, of remarking: "Where have we a dictatorship? Show it to me. It is confusion we have, but no dictatorship."

The word "confusion" he was very fond of.

"If we are not ready to shoot a saboteur and white guardist, what sort of big revolution is that? Just see how the bourgeois pack writes about us in the press! Where is there a dictatorship here? Nothing but talk and confusion ..." These speeches expressed his actual feeling, but at the same time they had a twofold end: according to his method Lenin hammered into the heads the consciousness that only unusually strong measures could save the revolution.

The weakness of the new state apparatus was most clearly manifest at the moment the Germans began the attack. "Yesterday we still sat firm in the saddle," said Lenin when alone with me, "and to-day we are only holding fast to the mane. But it is also a lesson. And this lesson cannot fail to have an effect upon our cursed negligence. To create order and really to attack the thing, is what we must do, if we do not wish to be enslaved! It will be a very good lesson if ... if only the Germans, along with the Whites, do not succeed in overthrowing us."

"Well," Vladimir Ilyich once asked me quite unexpectedly, "if the White Guards kill you and me will Bucharin come to an understanding with Sverdlof?"

"Perhaps they will not kill us," I answered jokingly.

"The devil knows," said Lenin and began to laugh himself. With that the conversation ended.

In one of the rooms at Smolny the staff held its sessions. It was the most confused of all the institutions. One never knew who made the arrangements, who commanded, and what was proper. Here was introduced for the first time the question of the military specialists in its general form. We had had some experience in this direction already in a struggle with Krasnov when we made Colonel Muravief commanding officer and he, on his side, appointed Colonel Walden to conduct the operations before Pulkoy. Four sailors and a soldier were sent to Muravief with instructions to be on guard and not to take their hands from their revolvers. That was the origin of the system of the Commissars. To a certain extent this experience was also the basis of the formation of the Supreme War Council.

"Without severity to presuming and experienced military men we will not get out of this chaos," I said to Vladimir Ilyich every time I had been to the staff.

"That is evidently right; but they will certainly make use of treachery."

"We must appoint a commissar for each one."

"You had better give them two," Lenin exclaimed, "and strong ones. But it cannot be that we have no strong communists."

Thus, began the formation of the Supreme War Council.

The question of the transfer of the government to Moscow caused no little friction. It seemed to be a desertion of Petrograd, which had laid the cornerstone of the October revolution. The workmen would not understand it. Smolny had become the symbol of the Soviet power and now they propose to liquidate it, etc.

Lenin was literally beside himself and replied to these objections: "Can you cover the question of the fate of the revolution with that kind of sentimental stupidity? If the Germans at a single bound take possession of Petersburg with us within it, the revolution is lost. If on the other hand the government is in Moscow, then the fall of Petersburg would only mean a serious part blow. How is it possible that you do not see and comprehend that? Besides if we stay in Petersburg under the present conditions, we increase its military danger and at the same time rouse the Germans to occupation of Petersburg. If on the contrary the government is in Moscow the temptation to take Petersburg is incomparably less. Is it any great advantage to occupy a hungry revolutionary city if this occupation does not decide the fate of the revolution and of peace? What is that stupid speech about the symbolic meaning of Smolny?

"Smolny is only Smolny because we are in it. And when we are in the Kremlin all their symbolism will be transferred to the Kremlin."

Finally the opposition was conquered. The government moved to Moscow. I remained in Petersburg for some time, I believe, as the president of the Petersburg revolutionary committee. On my arrival in Moscow I encountered Vladimir Ilyich in the Kremlin, in the so-called Cavaliers' wing. The "confusion," that is the disorder and chaos, were no less here than in Smolny. Vladimir Ilyich scolded good-naturedly about the Muscovites who fought for precedence, and he drew the reins tighter, step by step.

The government, which was renewed rather often in its separate parts, developed a feverish work in decrees. Every session of the Council of People's Commissars at first presented the picture of legislative improvisation on the greatest scale. Everything had to be begun at the beginning, had to be wrung from the ground. We could not offer "precedents," for history knew of none. Even simple requests were made difficult by the lack of time. The questions came up in progression of revolutionary inquisitiveness, that is, in incredible chaos. Big and little were mingled most remarkably. Less important practical problems led to the most involved questions of principle. Not all, by no means all, the decrees were in harmony, and Lenin joked more than once, even openly, at the discords in our product of decrees. But in the end these contradictions, even if uncouth viewed from the practical tasks of the moment, were lost sight of in the work of revolutionary thinking, that, by means of legislation, pointed out new ways for a new world of human relations.

It remains to be said that the direction of this whole work was incumbent upon Lenin. He presided unweariedly, five or six hours at a time, at the Council of People's Commissars – and these meetings took place daily at the first period – passed from question to question, led the debates, allotted the speakers time carefully by his watch, time that was later regulated by a presiding time-meter (or second-meter).

In general, the questions came up without any preparation, and they never could be postponed, as has already been stated. Very often the nature of the question, before the beginning of the debate, was unknown to the members of the Council of People's Commissars as well as to the president. But the discussions were always concise, the introductory report was given five to ten minutes.

None the less the president towed the meeting into the right channel. If the meeting was well attended and if there were any specialists and particularly any unknown persons among the participants, then Vladimir Ilyich resorted to one of his favorite gestures: he put his right hand before his forehead as a shield and looked through his fingers at the reporters and particularly at the members of the assembly, by which means, contrary to the expression "to look through the fingers," he watched very sharply and attentively. On a narrow strip of paper was posted in tiny letters (economy!) the list of speakers. One eye watched the time that was posted above the table every now and then, to remind the speaker it was time to stop. At the same time the President quickly made a note of the conclusions that had seemed to him especially important in the course of the debate, in the form of resolutions. Generally, in addition to this, Lenin, to save time, sent the assembly members short memoranda in which he asked for some kind of information. These notes would represent a very voluminous and very interesting epistolary element in the technique of soviet legislation, but a large part of them has been destroyed as the answer was written on the reverse side of the note which the President then carefully destroyed. At a definite time Lenin read aloud the resolution points, that were always intentionally stiff and pedagogic – in order to emphasize, to bring into prominence, to exclude any changes; then the debates were either at an end, or entered the concrete channel of practical motions and supplements. Lenin's "points" were thus the basis of the respective decree.

Among other necessary attributes this work required a strong creative imagination. This word may seem inadmissible at the first glance, but nevertheless it expresses exactly the essence of the thing. The human imagination may be of many kinds: the constructive engineer needs it as much as the unrestrained fiction writer. One of the most precious varieties of imagination consists in the ability to picture people, things, and phenomena as they are in reality, even when one has never seen them. The application and combination of the whole experience of life and theoretical equipment of a man with separate small stopping places caught in passing, their working up, fusion, and completion according to definite formulated laws of analogy, in order thereby to make clear a definite phase of human life in its whole concreteness – that is imagination, which is indispensable for a lawmaker, a government worker, and a leader in the time of revolution. The strength of Lenin lay, to a very important degree, in the strength of his realistic imagination.

Lenin's definiteness of purpose was always concrete, otherwise it would have belied its name. In the Iskra, I believe, Lenin for the first time expressed the thought, that in the complicated chain of political action one must always seek out the central link for the moment in question in order to seize it and give direction to the whole chain. Later, too, Lenin returned to this thought quite often, even to the same picture of the chain and the ring. This method passed from the sphere of the conscious, as it were, into his unconsciousness and finally became second nature. In particularly critical moments, when it was a question of a very responsible or risky tactical change of position, Lenin put aside everything else less important that permitted postponement. This must by no means be understood in the sense that he had grasped the central problem in its main features only and ignored details. Quite the contrary. He had before his eyes the problem that he considered could not be postponed, in all its concreteness, took hold of it from all sides, studied the details, now and then even the secondary ones, and sought a point of attack in order to approach it anew and give force to it, he recalled, expounded, emphasized, controlled, and urged. But all was subordinated to the "link of the chain" which he regarded as decisive for the moment in question. He put aside, not only all that was at variance, directly or indirectly, with the central problem, but also that which might distract his attention and weaken his exertion. In particularly critical moments he was likewise deaf and blind to everything that had nothing to do with the question which held his entire interest. Merely the raising of other questions, neutral ones so to speak, he felt as a danger from which he instinctively retreated.

When one critical step had been successfully overcome, Lenin would often exclaim for some cause or another: "But we have quite forgotten to do so and so ... We have made a mistake while we were entirely occupied with the main problem.

"They often answered: "But this question came up and exactly this proposition was made, only you would not hear anything of it then."

"Yes, really?" he would reply. "I do not remember at all."

Then he laughed slily and a little "consciously" and made a peculiar motion of the hand, characteristic of him, from above below, that seemed to mean: one cannot decide everything at the same time. This "defect" was only the reverse side of his faculty of the greatest inward mobilization of all his forces, and exactly this faculty made him the greatest revolutionary of history.

In Lenin's theses about peace written in January 1918, he says: **"For the success of socialism in Russia a certain period of time of at least a few months is necessary."**

Now these words seem quite incomprehensible. Is it not a mistake? Are not years or decades meant? But no, it is no mistake. One could probably find a number of other statements of Lenin of the same type. **I remember very well that in the first period, at the sessions of the Council of People's Commissars at Smolny,** Ilyich repeatedly said that **within a half year socialism would rule and that we would be the greatest state in the world.** The Left Social Revolutionaries, and not alone they, raised their heads in question and surprise, regarded each other, but were silent. This was his system of inculcation. Lenin wanted to train everybody, from now on, to consider all questions in the setting of their socialistic structure, not in the perspective of the "goal," but of today and tomorrow.

In this sharp change of position he seized the method so peculiar to him, of emphasizing the extreme: Yesterday we said socialism is the goal; but today it is a question of so thinking, speaking, and acting that the rule of socialism will be guaranteed in a few months. Does that mean too that it should be only a pedagogical method? No, not that alone. To the pedagogic energy something must be added: Lenin's strong idealism, his intense will-power, that in the sudden changes of two epochs shortened the stopping places, and drew nearer to the definite ends. He believed in what he said. And this imaginative half-year respite for the development of socialism just as much represents a function of Lenin's spirit as his realistic taking hold of every task of today. The deep and firm conviction of the strong possibilities of human development, for which one can and must pay any price whatsoever in sacrifices and suffering, was always the mainspring of Lenin's mental structure.

Under the most difficult circumstances, in the most wearing daily work, in the midst of commissariat troubles and all others possible, surrounded by a bourgeois war, Lenin worked with the greatest care over the Soviet constitution, scrupulously harmonized minor practical requisites of the state apparatus with the problems of principle of a proletarian dictatorship in a land of peasants.

The Constitution Commission decided for some reason or other to remodel Lenin's Declaration of the Rights of Producers and bring it into "accord" with the text of the constitution. When I came from the front to Moscow I received from the Commission, among other material, the outline of the transformed "declaration," or at least a part of it. I familiarized myself with it in Lenin's office, where only he and Sverdlof were present. They were doing the preparatory work for the Council of Soviets.

"But why is the declaration to be changed?" I asked Sverdlof, who was the head of the Constitution Commission.

Vladimir Ilyich raised his head with interest.

"Well, the Commission has just discovered that the 'declaration' contains discrepancies with the constitution and inexact formulations," Jakov Michailovich answered.

"In my opinion that is nonsense," I replied. "The declaration has already been accepted and has become an historical document – what sense is there in changing it?"

"That is quite right," Vladimir Ilyich interrupted. "I too think they have taken up this question quite unnecessarily. Let the youth live unshaven and disheveled: be he what he may, he is still a scion of the revolution ... he will hardly be better if you send him to the barber."

Sverdlof tried "dutifully" to stand by the decision of his Commission, but he soon agreed with us. I realized that Vladimir Ilyich, who more than once had had to oppose propositions of the Constitution Commission, apparently did not wish to take up the struggle against a rearrangement of the Declaration of the Righta of Producers, whose author he was. However, he was delighted by the support of a "third person" who unexpectedly turned up at the last moment. We three decided not to change the "declaration" and the worthy youth was spared the barber.

The study of the development of Soviet lawmaking in bringing into prominence its chief motives and turning points, in connection with the course of the revolution itself and the class relationships in it, presents a tremendously important task, because the results of it for the proletariat of other countries can be and must be of the greatest practical significance.

The collection of Soviet decrees forms, in a certain sense, a by no means unimportant part of the collected works of Vladimir Ilyich Lenin.

On the Slogan for a United States of Europe

August 23, 1915

Lenin Collected Work Volume 21, pages 339-343.

In No. 40 of Sotsial-Demokrat we reported that a conference of our-Party's groups abroad had decided to defer the question of the "United States of Europe" slogan pending a discussion, in the press, on the economic aspect of the matter.

At our conference the debate on this question assumed a purely political character. Perhaps this was partly caused by the Central Committee's Manifesto having formulated this slogan as a forthright political one ("the immediate political slogan...", as it says there); not only did it advance the slogan of a republican United States of Europe, but expressly emphasised that this slogan is meaningless and false "without the revolutionary overthrow of the German, Austrian and Russian monarchies".

It would be quite wrong to object to such a presentation of the question within the limits of a political appraisal of this slogan — e.g., to argue that it obscures or weakens, etc., the slogan of a socialist revolution. Political changes of a truly democratic nature, and especially political revolutions, can under no circumstances whatsoever either obscure or weaken the slogan of a socialist revolution. On the contrary, they always bring it closer, extend its basis, and draw new sections of the petty bourgeoisie and the semi-proletarian masses into the socialist struggle. On the other hand, political revolutions are inevitable in the course of the socialist revolution, which should not be regarded as a single act, but as a period of turbulent political and   economic upheavals, the most intense class struggle, civil war, revolutions, and counterrevolutions.

But while the slogan of a republican United States of Europe — if accompanied by the revolutionary overthrow of the three most reactionary monarchies in Europe, headed by the Russian—is quite invulnerable as a political slogan, there still remains the highly important question of its economic content and significance. From the standpoint of the economic conditions of imperialism—i.e., the export of capital and the division of the world by the "advanced" and "civilised" colonial powers—a United States of Europe, under capitalism, is either impossible or reactionary.

Capital has become international and monopolist. The world has been carved up by a handful of Great Powers, i.e., powers successful in the great plunder and oppression of nations. The four Great Powers of Europe—Britain, France, Russia and Germany, with an aggregate population of between 250,000,000 and 300,000,000, and an area of about 7,000,000 square kilometres—possess colonies with a population of almost 500 million (494,500,000) and an area of 64,600,000 square kilometres, i.e., almost half the surface of the globe (133,000,000 square kilometres, exclusive of Arctic and Antarctic regions). Add to this the three Asian states—China, Turkey and Persia, now being rent piecemeal by thugs that are waging a war of "liberation", namely, Japan, Russia, Britain and France. Those three Asian states, which may be called semi-colonies (in reality they are now 90 per cent colonies), have a total population of 360,000,000 and an area of 14,500,000 square kilometres (almost one and a half times the area of all Europe).

Furthermore, Britain, France and Germany have invested capital abroad to the value of no less than 70,000 million rubles. The business of securing "legitimate" profits from this tidy sum—these exceed 3,000 million rubles annually—committees of the millionaires, known as governments, which are equipped with armies and navies and which provide the sons and brothers of the millionaires with jobs in the colonies and semi-colonies as viceroys, consuls, ambassadors, officials of all kinds, clergymen, and other leeches.

That is how the plunder of about a thousand million of the earth's population by a handful of Great Powers is organised in the epoch of the highest development of capitalism. No other organisation is possible under capitalism. Renounce colonies, "spheres of influence", and the export of capital? To think that it is possible means coming down to the level of some snivelling parson who every Sunday preaches to the rich on the lofty principles of Christianity and advises them to give the poor, well, if not millions, at least several hundred rubles yearly.

A United States of Europe under capitalism is tantamount to an agreement on the partition of colonies. Under capitalism, however, no other basis and no other principle of division are possible except force. A multi-millionaire cannot share the "national income" of a capitalist country with anyone otherwise than "in proportion to the capital invested" (with a bonus thrown in, so that the biggest capital may receive more than its share). Capitalism is private ownership of the means of production, and anarchy in production. To advocate a "just" division of income on such a basis is sheer Proudhonism, stupid philistinism. No division can be effected otherwise than in "proportion to strength", and strength changes with the course of economic development. Following 1871, the rate of Germany's accession of strength was three or four times as rapid as that of Britain and France, and of Japan about ten times as rapid as Russia's. There is and there can be no other way of testing the real might of a capitalist state than by war. War does not contradict the fundamentals of private property—on the contrary, it is a direct and inevitable outcome of those fundamentals. Under capitalism the smooth economic growth of individual enterprises or individual states is impossible. Under capitalism, there are no other means of restoring the periodically disturbed equilibrium than crises in industry and wars in politics.

Of course, temporary agreements are possible between capitalists and between states. In this sense a United States of Europe is possible as an agreement between the European capitalists ... but to what end? Only for the purpose of jointly suppressing socialism in

Europe, of jointly protecting colonial booty against Japan and America, who have been badly done out of their share by the present partition of colonies, and the increase of whose might during the last fifty years has been immeasurably more rapid than that of backward and monarchist Europe, now turning senile. Compared with the United States of America, Europe as a whole denotes economic stagnation. On the present economic basis, i.e., under capitalism, a United States of Europe would signify an organisation of reaction to retard America's more rapid development. The times when the cause of democracy and socialism was associated only with Europe alone have gone forever.

A United States of the World (not of Europe alone) is the state form of the unification and freedom of nations which we associate with socialism—about the total disappearance of the state, including the democratic. As a separate slogan, however, the slogan of a United States of the World would hardly be a correct one, first, because it merges with socialism; second, because **it may be wrongly interpreted to mean that the victory of socialism in a single country is impossible**, and it may also **create misconceptions as to the relations of such a country to the others**.

Uneven economic and political development is an absolute law of capitalism. Hence, the victory of socialism is possible first in several or even in one capitalist country alone. After expropriating the capitalists and organising their own socialist production, the victorious proletariat of that country will arise against the rest of the world—the capitalist world—attracting to its cause the oppressed classes of other countries, stirring uprisings in those countries against the capitalists, and in case of need using even armed force against the exploiting classes and their states. The political form of a society wherein the proletariat is victorious in overthrowing the bourgeoisie will be a democratic republic, which will more and more concentrate the forces of the proletariat of a given nation or nations, in the struggle against states that have not yet gone over to socialism. The abolition of classes is impossible

37

without a dictatorship of the oppressed class, of the proletariat. A free union of nations in socialism is impossible without a more or less prolonged and stubborn   struggle of the socialist republics against the backward states.

It is for these reasons and after repeated discussions at the conference of R,S.D.L.P. groups abroad, and following that conference, that the Central Organ's editors have come to the conclusion that the slogan for a United States of Europe is an erroneous one.

Engels to Karl Kautsky

In Vienna

Abstract

London, 12 September 1882

You ask me what the English workers think about colonial policy. Well, exactly the same as they think about politics in general: the same as what the bourgeois think. There is no workers' party here, there are only Conservatives and Liberal-Radicals, and the workers gaily share the feast of England's monopoly of the world market and the colonies. In my opinion the colonies proper, i.e., the countries occupied by a European population, Canada, the Cape, Australia, will all become independent; on the other hand the countries inhabited by a native population, which are simply subjugated, India, Algiers, the Dutch, Portuguese and Spanish possessions, must be taken over for the time being by the proletariat and led as rapidly as possible towards independence. How this process will develop is difficult to say. India will perhaps, indeed very probably, produce a revolution, and as the proletariat emancipating itself cannot conduct any colonial wars, this would have to be given full scope; it would not pass off without all sorts of destruction, of course, but that sort of thing is inseparable from all revolutions. The same might also take place elsewhere, e.g., in Algiers and Egypt, and would certainly be the best thing for us. We shall have enough to do at home. Once Europe is reorganised, and North America, that will furnish such colossal power and such an example that the semi-civilised countries will follow in their wake of their own accord. Economic needs alone will be responsible for this. But as to what social and political phases these countries will then have to pass through before they likewise arrive at socialist organisation, we to-day can only advance rather idle hypotheses, I think. One thing alone is certain: **the victorious proletariat** can **force no blessings of any kind upon any foreign nation without**

undermining its own victory by so doing. Which of course by no means excludes defensive wars of various kinds.

The business in Egypt has been contrived by Russian diplomacy. Gladstone is to take Egypt (which he has not got yet by a long way and if he had it he would still be a long way from keeping it) in order that Russia may take Armenia, which according to Gladstone would be a further liberation of a Christian country from the Mohammedan yoke. Everything else about the affair is a sham, humbug, pretext. Whether the humbug will succeed will soon be seen.

Marx-Engels Correspondence 1882

The Military Programme of the Proletarian Revolution

September 1916
Lenin Collected Works, Moscow, Volume 23, pp.77-87.

Among the Dutch, Scandinavian and Swiss revolutionary Social-Democrats who are combating the social-chauvinist lies about "defence of the fatherland" in the present imperialist war, there have been voices in favour of replacing the old Social-Democratic minimum-programme demand for a "militia", or "the armed nation," by a new demand: "disarmament." The Jugend-Internationale has inaugurated a discussion on this issue and published, in No. 3, an editorial supporting disarmament. There is also, we regret to note, a concession to the "disarmament" idea in R. Grimm's latest theses. Discussion have been started in the periodicals Neue Leben and Vorbote.

Let us take a closer look at the position of the disarmament advocates.

Their principal argument is that the disarmament demand is the clearest, most decisive, most consistent expression of the struggle against all militarism and against all war.

But in this principal argument lies the disarmament advocates' principal error. Socialists cannot, without ceasing to be socialists, be opposed to all war.

Firstly, socialists have never been, nor can they ever be, opposed to revolutionary wars. The bourgeoisie of the imperialist "Great" Powers has become thoroughly reactionary, and the war this bourgeoisie is now waging we regard as a reactionary, slave-owners' and criminal war. But what about a war against this bourgeoisie? A war, for instance, waged by peoples oppressed by and dependent upon this bourgeoisie, or by colonial peoples, for liberation? In Section 5 of the Internationale group these we read:

"National wars are no longer possible in the era of this unbridled imperialism." That is obviously wrong.

The history of the 20th century, this century of "unbridled imperialism," is replete with colonial wars. But what we Europeans, the imperialist oppressors of the majority of the world's peoples, with our habitual, despicable European chauvinism, call "colonial wars" are often national wars, or national rebellions of these oppressed peoples. One of the main features of imperialism is that it accelerates capitalist development in the most backward countries, and thereby extends and intensifies the struggle against national oppression. That is a fact, and from it inevitably follows that imperialism must often give rise to national wars. Junius, who defends the above-quoted "theses" in her pamphlet, says that in the imperialist era every national war against an imperialist Great Power leads to intervention of a rival imperialist Great Power. Every national war is this turned into an imperialist war. But that argument is wrong, too. This can happen, but does not always happen. Many colonial wars between 1900 and 1914 did not follow that course. And it would be simply ridiculous to declare, for instance, that after the present war, if it ends in the utter exhaustion of all the belligerents, "there can be no" national, progress, revolutionary wars "of any kind", wages, say, by China in alliance with India, Persia, Siam, etc., against the Great Powers.

To deny all possibility of national wars under imperialism is wrong in theory, obviously mistaken historically, and tantamount to European chauvinism in practice: we who belong to nations that oppress hundreds of millions in Europe, Africa, Asia, etc., are invited to tell the oppressed peoples that it is "impossible" for them to wage war against "our" nations!

Secondly, civil war is just as much a war as any other. He who accepts the class struggle cannot fail to accept civil wars, which in every class society are the natural, and under certain conditions inevitable, continuation, development and intensification of the class struggle. That has been confirmed by every great revolution.

To repudiate civil war, or to forget about it, is to fall into extreme opportunism and renounce the socialist revolution.

Thirdly, **the victory of socialism in one country does not at one stroke eliminate all wars in general.** On the contrary, it presupposes wars. The development of capitalism proceeds extremely unevenly in different countries. It cannot be otherwise under commodity production. From this it follows irrefutably that socialism cannot achieve victory simultaneously in all countries. It will achieve victory first in one or several countries, while the others will for some time remain bourgeois or pre-bourgeois. This is bound to create not only friction, but a direct attempt on the part of the bourgeoisie of other countries to crush the socialist state's victorious proletariat. In such cases, a war on our part would be a legitimate and just war. It would be a war for socialism, for the liberation of other nations from the bourgeoisie. Engels was perfectly right when, in his letter to Kautsky of September 12, 1882, he clearly stated that it was possible for already victorious socialism to wage "defensive wars". What he had in mind was defense of the victorious proletariat against the bourgeoisie of other countries.

Only after we have overthrown, finally vanquished and expropriated the bourgeoisie of the whole world, and not merely in one country, will wars become impossible. And from a scientific point of view it would be utterly wrong—and utterly unrevolutionary—for us to evade or gloss over the most important things: crushing the resistance of the bourgeoisie—the most difficult task, and one demanding the greatest amount of fighting, in the transition to socialism. The "social" parsons and opportunists are always ready to build dreams of future peaceful socialism. But the very thing that distinguishes them from revolutionary Social-Democrats is that they refuse to think about and reflect on the fierce class struggle and class wars needed to achieve that beautiful future.

We must not allow ourselves to be led astray by words. The term "defense of the fatherland", for instance, is hateful to many because both avowed opportunists and Kautskyites use it to cover up and gloss over the bourgeois lie about the present predatory war. This is a fact. But it does not follow that we must no longer see through to the meaning of political slogans. To accept "defense of the fatherland" in the present war is no more nor less than to accept it as a "just" war, a war in the interests of the proletariat—no more nor less, we repeat, because invasions may occur in any war. It would be sheer folly to repudiate "defense of the fatherland" on the part of oppressed nations in their wars against the imperialist Great Powers, or on the part of a victorious proletariat in its war against some Galliffet of a bourgeois state.

Theoretically, it would be absolutely wrong to forget that every war is but the continuation of policy by other means. The present imperialist war is the continuation of the imperialist policies of two groups of Great Powers, and these policies were engendered and fostered by the sum total of the relationships of the imperialist era. But this very era must also necessarily engender and foster policies of struggle against national oppression and of proletarian struggle against the bourgeoisie and, consequently, also the possibility and inevitability; first, of revolutionary national rebellions and wars; second, of proletarian wars and rebellions against the bourgeoisie; and, third, of a combination of both kinds of revolutionary war, etc.

The "Disarmament" Slogan

October 1916

Lenin Collected Works, Volume 23, pages 94-104.

Let us take a closer look at the position of the disarmament advocates.

One of the principal premises advanced, although not always definitely expressed, in favour of disarmament is this: we are opposed to war, to all war in general, and the demand for disarmament, is the most definite, clear and unambiguous expression of this point of view.

We showed the fallacy of that idea in our review of Junius's pamphlet, to which we refer the reader. **Socialists cannot be opposed to all war in general without ceasing to be socialists**. We must not allow ourselves to be blinded by the present imperialist war. Such wars between "Great" Powers are typical of the imperialist epoch; but democratic wars and rebellions, for instance, of oppressed nations against their oppressors to free themselves from oppression, are by no means impossible. Civil wars of the proletariat against the bourgeoisie for socialism are inevitable. Wars are possible between **one country in which socialism has been victorious** and other, bourgeois or reactionary, countries.

Disarmament is the ideal of socialism. There will be no wars in socialist society; consequently, disarmament will be achieved. But whoever expects that socialism will be achieved without a social revolution and the dictatorship of the proletariat is not a socialist. Dictatorship is state power based directly on violence. And in the twentieth century—as in the age of civilisation generally—violence means neither a fist nor a club, but troops. To put "disarmament" in the programme is tantamount to making the general declaration: We are opposed to the use of arms. There is as little Marxism in this as there would be if we were to say: We are opposed to violence!

It should be observed that the international discussion of this question was conducted mainly, if not exclusively, in the German language. The Germans, however, use two words, the difference between which is not easily rendered in Russian. One, strictly speaking, means "disarmament",[2] and is used by Kautsky and the Kautskyites, for instance, in the sense of reduction of armaments. The other, strictly speaking, means "disarming",[3] and is used mainly by the Lefts in the sense of abolishing militarism, abolishing all militarist systems. In this article we speak of the latter demand, which is current among certain revolutionary Social-Democrats.

The Kautskyite advocacy of "disarmament", which is addressed to the present governments of the imperialist Great Powers, is the most vulgar opportunism, it is bourgeois pacifism, which actually—in spite of the "good intentions" of the sentimental Kautskyites—serves to distract the workers from the revolutionary struggle. For this advocacy seeks to instill in the workers the idea that the present bourgeois governments of the imperialist powers are not bound to each other by thousands of threads of finance capital and by scores or hundreds of corresponding secret treaties (i.e., predatory, plundering treaties, preparing the way for imperialist war).

Report On The Activities Of The Council Of People's Commissars

January 14(24)
Lenin Collected Works, Volume 26, 1972, pp. 453-482

Comrades, on behalf of the Council of People's Commissars I must submit to you a report of its activities for the two months and fifteen days that have elapsed since the establishment of Soviet power and the Soviet Government in Russia.

Two months and fifteen days—that is only five days more than the preceding workers' power lasted and ruled over a whole country, or over the exploiters and the capitalists, the power of the Paris workers at the time of the Paris Commune of 1871.

We must first of all remember this workers' power, we must cast our minds back and compare it with the Soviet power that was formed on October 25. And if we compare the preceding dictatorship of the proletariat with the present one we shall see at once what a gigantic stride the international working-class movement has made, and in what an immeasurably more favourable position Soviet power in Russia finds itself, notwithstanding the incredibly complicated conditions of war and economic ruin.

After retaining power for two months and ten days, the workers of Paris, who for the first time in history established the Commune, the embryo of Soviet power, perished at the hands of the French Cadets, Mensheviks and Right Socialist-Revolutionaries of a Kaledin type. The French workers had to pay an unprecedentedly heavy price for the first experience of workers' government, the meaning and purpose of which the overwhelming majority of the peasants in France did not know.

We find ourselves in immeasurably more favourable circumstances because the Russian soldiers, workers and peasants were able 'to create the Soviet Government, an apparatus which informed the whole world of their methods of struggle. It is this that puts the Russian workers and peasants in a position that differs from the power of the Paris proletariat. They had no apparatus, the country did not understand them; we were immediately able to rely on Soviet power, and that is why we never doubted that Soviet power enjoys the sympathy and the warmest and most devoted support of the overwhelming majority of the people, and that therefore Soviet power is invincible.

Those who were sceptical of Soviet power and frequently, either consciously or unconsciously, sold and betrayed it for compromise with the capitalists and the imperialists, raised a deafening clamour about the power of the proletariat alone not being able to be maintained in Russia. As if any Bolsheviks or their supporters forgot even for a moment that in Russia only that power could last for any length of time that would be able to unite the working class and the majority of the peasants, all the working and exploited classes, in a single, inseparably interconnected force fighting against the landowners and the bourgeoisie.

We never doubted that only the alliance of the workers and the poor peasants, the semi-proletarians, mentioned in our Party Programme, can, in Russia, embrace the majority of the population arid ensure firm support for the government. And after October 25 we were immediately able, in the course of several weeks, to overcome all difficulties and establish a government on the basis of this firm alliance.

Yes, comrades! When the Socialist-Revolutionary Party, in its old form—when the peasants did not yet understand who in this party were real advocates of socialism—put forward the slogan of egalitarian land tenure, without caring who was to put it through, whether it was to be effected in alliance with the bourgeoisie or not, we branded that as a fraud. And this section, which has now realised that the people are not with it and that it is a bubble, claimed that it could carry out egalitarian land tenure in alliance

48

with the bourgeoisie. In this lay the basic fraud. And when the Russian revolution presented an example of collaboration between the working people and the bourgeoisie, in the greatest moment in the life of the people; when the war had been ruining the people and dooming millions to death from starvation and its consequences showed what compromise meant in practice; when the Soviets themselves experienced it and felt it after having passed through the school of compromise, it became obvious that there was a sound, virile and great socialist core in the teachings of those who wanted to unite the working section of the peasants with the great socialist movement of the workers of the whole world.

And as soon as this became a clear and distinct practical question to the peasants, something happened of which no one had any doubt, as has now been proved by the Peasants' Soviets and Congresses: when the time came to implement socialism, the peasants were able to see clearly these two main political lines— alliance with the bourgeoisie, or alliance with the working people. They then realised that the party which expressed the real aims and interests of the peasants was the Left Socialist-Revolutionary Party. And when we concluded our government alliance with this party, we, from the very outset, arranged it so that the alliance rested on the clearest and most obvious principles. If the peasants of Russia want to socialise the land in alliance with the workers who will nationalise the banks and establish workers' control, then they are our loyal colleagues, our most loyal and valuable allies. Comrades, no socialist would refuse to admit the obvious truth that between socialism and capitalism there lies a long, more or less difficult transitional period of the dictatorship of the proletariat, and that the forms this period will take will be determined to a large extent by whether small or big ownership, small or large-scale farming, predominates. It goes without saying that the transition to socialism in Estland, that small country in which the whole population is literate, and which consists of large-scale farms, cannot be the same as the transition to socialism in Russia, which is mainly a petty-bourgeois country. This must be taken into account.

Every politically-conscious socialist says that socialism cannot be imposed upon the peasants by force and that we must count only on the power of example and on the mass of the peasants assimilating day-to-day experience. How would the peasants prefer to pass to socialism? This is the problem which now confronts the Russian peasants in practice. How can they support the socialist proletariat and begin the transition to socialism? The peasants have already tackled this transition, and we have complete confidence in them.

The alliance we concluded with the Left Socialist-Revolutionaries is built on a firm basis and is growing stronger and stronger by the hour. At first we on the Council of People's Commissars feared that factional struggle would hinder the work, but now, after the experience of two months' work together, I must say definitely that on the majority of questions we arrive at unanimous decisions.

We know that only when experience has shown the peasants, for example, the kind of exchange there must be between town and country they will themselves, from below, on the basis of their own experience, establish their own connections. On the other hand, the experience of the Civil War has demonstrated to the peasants that there is no other road to socialism except the dictatorship of the proletariat and the ruthless suppression of the rule of the exploiters. (Applause)

Comrades, every time we touch upon this theme, at the present meeting, or in the Central Executive Committee, I, from time to time, hear from the Right side of the meeting the exclamation "Dictator!" Yes, "when we were socialists" everyone recognised the dictatorship of the proletariat; they even wrote about it in their programmes, they were indignant at the widespread false idea that it was possible to persuade and prove to the population that the working people ought not to be exploited, that this was sinful and disgraceful, and that once people were persuaded of this there would be paradise on earth. No, this utopian notion was smashed in theory long ago, and now our task is to smash it in practice.

We must not depict socialism as if socialists will bring it to us on a plate all nicely dressed. That will never happen. Not a single problem of the class struggle has ever been solved in history except by violence. When violence is exercised by the working people, by the mass of exploited against the exploiters—then we are for it! (Stormy applause.) And we are not in the least disturbed by the howls of those people who consciously or unconsciously side with the bourgeoisie, or who are so frightened by them, so oppressed by their rule, that they have been flung into consternation at the sight of this unprecedentedly acute class struggle, have burst into tears, forgotten all their premises and demand that we perform the impossible, that we socialists achieve complete victory without fighting against the exploiters and without suppressing their resistance.

As far back as the summer of 1917 the exploiters understood that it is a matter of "the last and decisive battles", and that if the Soviets came to power the last bulwark of the bourgeoisie, their principal source for suppressing the working people, would be torn out of their hands.

That is why the October Revolution began this systematic and unswerving struggle to compel the exploiters to cease their resistance and to become reconciled to the idea, no matter how difficult that may be for even the best of them, that the rule of the exploiting classes has gone never to return, that from now on the ordinary peasant will give the orders and that they must obey, however unpleasant that may be.

This will entail many difficulties, sacrifices and mistakes; it is something new, unprecedented in history and cannot be studied from books. It goes without saying that this is the greatest and most difficult transition that has ever occurred in history; but there is no other way to make this great transition and the fact that Soviet power has been established in Russia has shown that it is the revolutionary people who are richest of all in revolutionary experience—when millions come to the assistance of a few score of

Party people—the people who actually take their exploiters by the throat.

That is why civil war has acquired predominance in Russia at the present time. Against us is advanced tile slogan: "Down with civil war!" I happened to hear this shouted from the Bight benches of the so-called Constituent Assembly. Down with civil war.... What does that mean? Civil war against whom? Against Kornilov, Kerensky and Byabushinsky who are spending millions to bribe vagabonds and officials? Against the saboteurs who, consciously or unconsciously, are accepting these bribes? Undoubtedly, among the latter there are ignorant people who accept these bribes unconsciously, because they cannot even imagine that the old bourgeois system can and must be destroyed to the very foundation and that an entirely new, socialist society can and must be built up on its ruins. Undoubtedly there are people like that, but does that alter the situation?

That is why the representatives of the propertied classes are staking their all, that is why these are the last and decisive battles for them, and they would stop at no crime in their efforts to smash Soviet power. Does not the whole history of socialism, particularly of French socialism, which is so rich in revolutionary striving, show us that when the working people themselves take power in their hands the ruling classes resort to unheard-of crimes and shootings if it is a matter of protecting their money-bags. When these people talk to us about civil war we answer them with ridicule; but when they spread their slogans among the students we say—you are deceiving them!

The class struggle did not accidentally assume its latest form, the form in which the exploited class takes all the means of power in its own hands in order to completely destroy its class enemy, the bourgeoisie, in order to sweep from the land of Russia not only the bureaucrats, but also the landowners, as the Russian peasants in several gubernias have done.

We are told that the sabotage with which the bureaucrats and the landowners met the Council of People's Commissars is an indication of their unwillingness to assist socialism, as if it were not clear that the whole of this gang of capitalists and swindlers, vagabonds and saboteurs, represent a single gang bribed by the bourgeoisie and resisting the power of the working people. Of course, those who thought that it was possible to leap straight from capitalism to socialism, or those who imagined that it was possible to convince the majority of the population that this could be achieved through the medium of the Constituent Assembly—those who believed in this bourgeois-democratic fable, can go on blithely believing it, but let them not complain if life destroys this fable.

Those who have come to understand what the class struggle means, what the sabotage organised by the bureaucrats means, know that we cannot leap straight into socialism. There remained the bourgeoisie, capitalists, who hope to restore their rule and who defend their money-bags. There remained vagabonds, a section of corrupt people who are absolutely downtrodden by capitalism and who are unable to grasp the idea of the proletarian struggle. There remained office employees, bureaucrats who believe that it is in the interests of society to protect the old system. how can anyone imagine that the victory of socialism can come about except by the complete collapse of these sections, except by the complete destruction of the Russian and European bourgeoisie? Do you think the Ryabushinskys do not understand their class interests? It is they who are paying the saboteurs not to work. Or do they operate disunited? Are they not operating in conjunction with the French, British and American capitalists by buying up securities? It remains to be seen whether they will get much out of these transactions. Will not the heaps of securities they are now buying up turn out to be merely useless heaps of scrap-paper?

That is why, comrades, our reply to all the reproaches and accusations hurled against us of employing terror, dictatorship, civil war, although we are far from having resorted to real terror, because we are stronger than they— we have the Soviets, it will be sufficient if we nationalise the banks and confiscate their property in order to compel them to submit—our reply to all these charges of instigating civil war is: yes, we have openly proclaimed what no other government has been able to proclaim. The first government in the world that can speak openly of civil war is the government of the workers, peasants and soldiers. Yes, we have started and we are waging civil war against the exploiters. The more straightforwardly we say this, the more quickly will this war come to an end, the more quickly will all the working and exploited people understand us, will understand that Soviet power is fighting for the real, vital cause of all the working people.

Comrades, I do not think we shall achieve victory in this struggle quickly, but we are very rich in experience: we have managed to achieve a great deal in the course of two months. We have experienced Kerensky's attempt to launch an attack against Soviet power and the complete failure of this attempt. We have experienced the organisation of power of the Ukrainian Kerenskys—t.he struggle has not yet ended there, but to anyone who has watched it., who has heard at least a few truthful reports from representatives of Soviet power, it is obvious that tile bourgeois elements of the Ukrainian Rada are living their last days. (Applause) There cannot be the slightest doubt about the victory of Soviet power, of the Ukrainian People's Republic, over the Ukrainian bourgeois Rada.

As for the struggle against Kaledin—here, indeed, everything rests on the basis of the exploitation of the working people, on the basis of the bourgeois dictatorship—if there is any social basis at all against Soviet power. The Peasants' Congress has clearly demonstrated that Kaledin's cause is hopeless; the working people are against him. The experience of Soviet power, propaganda by deeds, by the example of the Soviet organisations, is having its effect, and Kaledin's stronghold in the Don Region is how collapsing—not so much externally as internally.

That is why, looking at the civil war front in Russia, we can say with complete conviction: here the victory of Soviet power is complete and absolutely assured. And, comrades, the victory of Soviet power is being achieved because right from the outset it began to realise the age-old aspirations of socialism, while consistently and determinedly relying on the people and considering it to be its duty to awaken the most oppressed and downtrodden sections of society to active life, to raise them to socialist creative work. That is why the old army with its barrack-square drilling and torture of soldiers has retreated into the past. It has been thrown on the scrap-heap, nothing remains of it. (Applause) The complete democratisation of the army has been carried out.

Permit me to relate an incident that occurred when I was in the carriage of a Finnish train and I overheard a conversation between several Finns and an old woman. I could not take part in the conversation because I cannot speak Finnish. But one of the Finns turned to me and said: "Do you know the curious thing this old woman said? She said, 'Now there is no need to fear the man with the gun. I was in the woods one day and I met a man with a gun, and instead of taking the firewood I had collected from me, he added some more.'"

When I heard that, I said to myself: let the hundreds of newspapers, no matter what they call themselves—socialist, near-socialist, etc.— let hundreds of extremely loud voices shout at us, "dictators", "violators", and similar words. We know that another voice is now rising from among the people; they say to themselves: now we need not be afraid of the man with the gun because he protects the working people and will be ruthless in suppressing the rule of the exploiters. (Applause) This is what the people have felt, and that is why the propaganda that simple and uneducated people are carrying on when they relate how the Red Guardsare turning their might against the exploiters—that propaganda is invincible. It will spread among millions and tens of millions, and will firmly create what the French Commune of the nineteenth century began to create, but was able to continue for only a very short time because it was wrecked by the bourgeoisie—it will create a socialist Red Army, something all socialists have always aimed at, i.e., the general arming of the people. It will create new Red Guard cadres that will enable us to train the working people for the armed struggle.

It used to be said about Russia that she would be unable to fight because she would have no officers. But we must not forget what these very bourgeois officers said as they observed the workers fighting against Kerensky and Kaledin. They said: "The Red Guards' technical level is very low, but if these people had a little training they would have an invincible army." This is because, for the first time in the history of the world struggle, elements have entered the army which are not the vehicles of bureaucratic knowledge, but are guided by the idea of the struggle to emancipate the exploited. And when the work we have commenced is completed, the Russian Soviet Republic will be invincible. (Applause)

Comrades, the road which Soviet power has traversed insofar as concerns the socialist army has also been traversed insofar as concerns another instrument of the ruling classes, an even more subtle, an even more complicated instrument—the bourgeois court, which claimed to maintain order, but which, as a matter of fact, was a blind, subtle instrument for the ruthless suppression of the exploited, an(h an instrument for protecting the interests of the moneybags. Soviet power acted in the way all the proletarian revolutions had shown that it must act; it immediately threw the 01(1 court on to the scrap-heap. Let them shout that we, without reforming the old court, immediately threw it on to the scrap-heap. By that we paved the way for a real people's court, and not so much by the force of repressive measures as by massive example, the authority of the working people, without formalities; we transformed the court from an instrument of exploitation into an instrument of education on the firm foundations of socialist society. There is no doubt whatever that we cannot attain such a society at once.

These, then, are the main steps Soviet power has taken along the road indicated by the experience of the great popular revolutions throughout the world. There has not been a single revolution in which the working people did not begin to take some steps along this road in order to set up a new state power. Unfortunately, they only began to do this, but were unable to finish, they were unable to create the new type of state power. We have created it—we have already established a socialist Republic of Soviets.

I have no illusions about our having only just entered the period of transition to socialism, about not yet having reached socialism. But if you say that our state is a socialist Republic of Soviets, you will be right. You will be as right as those who call many Western bourgeois republics democratic republics although everybody knows that not one of even the most democratic of these republics is completely democratic. They grant scraps of democracy, they cut off tiny bits of the rights of the exploiters, but the working people are as much oppressed there as they are everywhere else. Nevertheless, we say that the bourgeois system is represented by both old monarchies and by constitutional republics.

And so in our case now. We are far from having completed even the transitional period from capitalism to socialism. We have never cherished the hope that we could finish it without the aid of the international proletariat. We never had any illusions on that score, and we know how difficult is the road that leads from capitalism to socialism. But it is our duty to say that our Soviet Republic is a socialist republic because we have taken this road, and our words will riot be empty words.

We have initiated many measures undermining the capitalists' rule. We know that our power had to unite the activities of all our institutions by a single principle, and this principle we express in the words: "Russia is declared to be a Socialist Republic of Soviets." (Applause) This will be that truth which rests on what we must do and have already begun to do, this will be the best unification of all our activities, the proclamation of our programme, a call to the working people and the exploited of all countries who either do not know at all what socialism is, or, what is worse, believe that socialism is the Chernov-Tsereteli mess of bourgeois reforms which we have tasted and tried during the ten months of the revolution and which we have become convinced is a falsification and not socialism.

And that is why 'free" Britain and France did all they could during the ten months of our revolution to prevent a single copy of Bolshevik and Left Socialist-Revolutionary newspapers from entering their countries. They had to act in this way because they saw that the workers and peasants in all countries instinctively grasped what the Russian workers were doing. There was not a single meeting where news about the Russian revolution and the slogan of Soviet power was not hailed with stormy applause. The working people and the exploited everywhere have already come into conflict with their party top leadership. The old socialism of these leaders is not yet buried like that of Chkheidze and Tsereteli in Russia, but it is already done for in all countries of the world, it is already dead.

A new state—the Republic of Soviets, the republic of the working people, of the exploited classes that are breaking down the old bourgeois barriers, now stands against the old bourgeois system. New state forms have been created, which make it possible to suppress the exploiters, to overcome the resistance of this insignificant handful who are still strong because of yesterday's money-bags and yesterday's store of knowledge. They—the professors, teachers and engineers—transform their knowledge into an instrument for the exploitation of the working people, saying they want their knowledge to serve the bourgeoisie, otherwise they refuse to work. But their power has been broken by the workers' and peasants' revolution, and a state is rising against them in which the people themselves freely elect their own representatives.

It is precisely at the present time that we can say that we really have- an organisation of power which clearly indicates the transition to the complete abolition of any power, of any state. This will be possible when every trace of exploitation has been abolished, that is, in socialist society.

Now I shall deal briefly with the measures which the socialist Soviet Government of Russia has begun to realise. The nationalisation of the banks was one of the first measures adopted for the purpose, not only of wiping the landowners from the face of Russian earth, but also of eradicating the rule of the bourgeoisie and the possibility of capital oppressing millions and tens of millions of the working people. The banks are important centres of modern capitalist economy. They collect fantastic wealth and distribute it over this vast country; they are the nerve centres of capitalist life. They are subtle and intricate organisations, which grew up in the course of centuries; and against them were hurled the first blows of Soviet power which at first encountered desperate resistance in the State Bank. But this resistance did not deter Soviet power. We succeeded in the main thing, in organising the State Bank; this main thing is in the hands of the workers and peasants. After these basic measures, which still require a lot of working out in detail, we proceeded to lay our hands on the private banks.

We did not act in the way the compromisers would probably have recommended us to do, i.e., first wait until the Constituent Assembly is convened, then perhaps draft a bill and introduce it in the Constituent Assembly and by that inform the bourgeoisie of our intentions and enable them to find a loophole through which to extricate themselves from this unpleasant thing; perhaps draw them into our company, and then make state laws—that would be a "state act".

That would be the rejection of socialism. We acted quite simply; not fearing to call forth the reproaches of the "educated" people, or rather of the uneducated supporters of the bourgeoisie who were trading in the remnants of their knowledge, we said we had at our disposal armed workers and peasants. This morning they must occupy all the private banks. (Applause) After they have done that, after power is in our hands, only after this, we shall discuss what measures to adopt. In the morning, the banks were occupied and in the evening the Central Executive Committee issued a decree: "The banks are declared national property"— state control, the socialisation of banking, its transfer to Soviet power, took place.

There was not a man among us who could imagine that an intricate and subtle apparatus like banking, which grew out of the capitalist system of economy in the course of centuries, could be broken or transformed in a few days. We never said that. And when scientists, or pseudo-scientists, shook their heads and prophesied, we said: you can prophesy what you like. We know only one way for the proletarian revolution, namely, to occupy the enemy's positions-to learn to rule by experience, from our mistakes. We do not in the least belittle the difficulties in our path, but we have done the main thing. The source of capitalist wealth has been undermined in the place of its distribution. After all this, the repudiation of the state loans, the overthrow of the financial yoke, was a very easy step. The transition to confiscation of the factories, after workers' control had been introduced, was also very easy. When we were accused of breaking up production into separate departments by introducing workers' control, we brushed aside this nonsense. In introducing workers' control, we knew that it would take much time before it spread to the whole of Russia, but we wanted to show that we recognise only one road —changes from below; we wanted the workers themselves, from below, to draw up the new, basic economic principles. Much time will be required for this.

From workers' control we passed on to the creation of a Supreme Economic Council. Only this measure, together with the nationalisation of the banks and railways which will be carried out within the next few days, will make it possible for us to begin work to build up a new socialist economy. We know perfectly well the difficulties that confront us in this work; but we assert that only those who set to work to carry out this task relying on the experience and the instinct of the working people are socialists indeed. The people will commit many mistakes, but the main thing has been done. They know that when they appeal to Soviet power, they will get whole-hearted support against the exploiters. There is not a single measure intended to ease their work that was not entirely supported by Soviet power. Soviet power does not know everything and cannot handle everything in time, and very often it is confronted with difficult tasks. Very often delegations of workers and peasants come to the government and ask, for example, what to do with such-and-such a piece of land. And frequently I myself have felt embarrassed when I saw that they had no very definite views. And I said to them: you are the power, do all you want to do, take all you want, we shall support you, but take care of production, see that production is useful. Take up useful work, you will make mistakes, but you will learn. And the workers have already begun to learn; they have already begun to fight against the saboteurs. Education has been turned into a fence which hinders the advance of the working classes; it will be pulled down.

Undoubtedly, the war is corrupting people both in the rear and at the front; people who are working on war supplies are paid far above the rates, and this attracts all those who hid themselves to keep out of the war, the vagabond and semi-vagabond elements who are imbued with one desire, to "grab" something and clear out. But these elements are the worst that has remained of the old capitalist system and are the vehicles of all the old evils; these we must kick out, remove, and we must put in the factories all the best proletarian elements and form them into nuclei of future socialist Russia. This is not an easy task, it will give rise to many conflicts, too much friction and many clashes. We, the Council of People's Commissars, and I personally, have heard complaints and threats from them, but we have remained calm, knowing that now we have a judge to whom we can appeal. That judge is the Soviets of Workers' and Soldiers' Deputies. (Applause). The word of this judge is indisputable, and we shall always rely upon it.

Capitalism deliberately differentiates the workers in order to rally an insignificant handful of the upper section of the working class around the bourgeoisie. Conflicts with this section are inevitable. We shall not achieve socialism without a struggle. But we are ready to fight, we have started it and we shall finish it with the aid of the apparatus called the Soviets. The Soviet of Workers' and Soldiers' Deputies will easily solve any problem we bring before it. For however strong the group of privileged workers may be, when they are brought before the representative body of all the workers, then this court, I repeat, will be indisputable for them. This sort of adjustment is only just beginning. The workers and peasants have not yet sufficient confidence in their own strength; age-old tradition has made them far too used to waiting for orders from above. They have not yet fully appreciated the fact that the proletariat is the ruling class; there are still elements among them who are frightened and downtrodden and who imagine that they must pass through the despicable school of the bourgeoisie. This most despicable of bourgeois notions has remained alive longer than all the rest, but it is dying and will die out completely. And we are convinced that with every step Soviet power takes the number of people will constantly grow who have completely thrown off the old bourgeois notion that a simple worker and peasant cannot administer the state. Well, if he sets to doing it, he can and will learn! (Applause).

And it will be our organisational task to select leaders and organisers from among the people. This enormous, gigantic work is now on the agenda. There could even be no thought of carrying it out if it were not for Soviet power, a filtering apparatus which can promote people.

Not only have we a state law on control, we have something even far more valuable — attempts on the part of the proletariat to enter into agreements with the manufacturers' associations in order to guarantee the workers' management over whole branches of industry. Such an agreement has begun to be drawn up, and is almost completed, between the leather workers and the all-Russia leather manufacturers' society. I attach very special importance to these agreements; they show that the workers are becoming aware of their strength.

Comrades, in my report I have not dealt with the particularly painful and difficult questions of peace and the food supply, because they are special items on the agenda and will be discussed separately.

My purpose in making this brief report was to show, as it appears to me and to the whole of the Council of People's Commissars, the entire history of what we have experienced during the past two and a half months, how the relation of class forces took shape in this new period of the Russian revolution, how a new state power was formed and what social tasks confront it.

Russia has started to achieve socialism in the right way— by the nationalisation of the banks and the transfer of all the land entirely to the working people. We are well aware of the difficulties that lie ahead, but we are convinced, by comparing our revolution with previous revolutions, that we shall achieve enormous successes and that we are on the road that guarantees complete victory.

And with us will go the masses of the more advanced countries, countries which have been divided by a predatory war, whose workers have passed through a longer period of training in democracy. When people depict the difficulties of our task, **when we are told that the victory of socialism is possible only on a world scale,** we regard this merely as an attempt, **a particularly hopeless attempt, on the part of the bourgeoisie and of its voluntary and involuntary supporters to distort the irrefutable truth.** The **final victory** of socialism in a single country is of course impossible. Our contingent of workers and peasants which is upholding Soviet power is one of the contingents of the great world army, which at present has been split by the world war, but which is striving for unity, and every piece of information, every fragment of a report about our revolution, every name, the proletariat greets with loud and sympathetic cheers, because it knows that in Russia the common cause is being pursued, the cause of the proletariat's uprising, the international socialist revolution. A living example, tackling the job somewhere in one country is more effective than any proclamations and conferences; this is what inspires the working people in all countries.

The October strike in 1905—the first steps of the victorious revolution—immediately spread to Western Europe and then, in 1905, called forth the movement of the Austrian workers; already at that time we had a practical illustration of the value of the example of revolution, of the action by the workers in one country, and today we see that the socialist revolution is maturing by the hour in all countries of the world.

If we make mistakes and blunders and meet with obstacles on our way, that is not what is important to them; what is important to them is our example, that is what unites them. They say: we shall go together and conquer, come what may. (Applause).

The great founders of socialism, Marx and Engels, having watched the development of the labour movement and the growth of the world socialist revolution for a number of decades saw clearly that the transition from capitalism to socialism would require prolonged birth-pangs, a long period of the dictatorship of the proletariat, the break-up of all that belonged to the past, the ruthless destruction of all forms of capitalism, the co.-operation of the workers of all countries, who would have to combine their efforts to ensure complete victory. And they said that at the end of the nineteenth century "the Frenchman will begin it, and the German will finish it" —.the Frenchman would begin it because in the course of decades of revolution he had acquired that intrepid initiative in revolutionary action that made him the vanguard of the socialist revolution.

Today we see a different combination of international socialist forces. We say that it is easier for the movement to start in the countries that are not among those exploiting countries which have opportunities for easy plunder and are able to bribe the upper section of their workers. The pseudo-socialist, nearly all ministerial, Chernov-Tsereteli parties of Western Europe do not accomplish anything, and they lack firm foundations. We have seen the example of Italy; during the past few days we witnessed the heroic struggle of the Austrian workers against the predatory imperialists.185 Though the pirates may succeed in holding up the movement for a time, they cannot stop it altogether, it is invincible.

The example of the Soviet Republic will stand before them for a long time to come. Our socialist Republic of Soviets will stand secure, as a torch of international socialism and as an example to all the working people. Over there—conflict, war, bloodshed, the sacrifice of millions of people, capitalist exploitation; here—a genuine policy of peace and a socialist Republic of Soviets.

Things have turned out differently from what Marx and Engels expected and we, the Russian working and exploited classes, have the honour of being the vanguard of the international socialist revolution; we can now see clearly how far the development of the revolution will go. The Russian began it—the German, the Frenchman and the Englishman will finish it, and socialism will be victorious. (Applause)

Report On Foreign Policy

Lenin
Speech Delivered At A Joint Meeting Of The All-Russia Central
Executive Committee And The Moscow Soviet
May 14, 1918

Lenin Collected Works, Volume 27, pages 365-381

Comrades, permit me to acquaint you with the present foreign
policy situation. In the past few days our international position has
in many respects become more complicated owing to the
aggravation of the general situation. Because of this aggravation,
the provocation, the deliberate panic-spreading by the bourgeois
press and its echo, the socialist press, is again doing its dark and
filthy work of repeating the Kornilov affair.

First, I shall draw your attention to the factors determining, in the
main, the international position of the Soviet Republic in order to
proceed to the outward legal forms determining this position, and,
on the basis of this, describe again the difficulties which have arisen
or, to be more precise, define the turning-point at which we have
arrived and which forms the basis of the worsened political
situation.

Comrades, you know, and your knowledge has been particularly
reinforced by the experience of the two Russian revolutions, that
economic interests and the economic position of the classes which
rule our state lie at the root of both our home and foreign policy.
These propositions which constitute the basis of the Marxist world
outlook and have been confirmed for us Russian revolutionaries by
the great experience of both Russian revolutions, must not be
forgotten even for a moment if we are to avoid losing ourselves in
the thickets, the labyrinth of diplomatic tricks, a labyrinth which at
times is artificially created and made more intricate by people,
classes, parties and groups who like to fish in muddy waters, or
who are compelled to do so.

We recently experienced, and to a certain extent are experiencing now, a situation in which our counter-revolutionaries—the Constitutional-Democrats and their foremost yes-men, the Right Socialist-Revolutionaries and Mensheviks—have been attempting to take advantage of the increased complexity of the international situation.

Basically, the position is that the Russian Socialist Soviet Republic, due to economic and political causes which we have described in the press on more than one occasion, and of which you are aware, due to a different rate of development, a basis of development different from that of the West, still remains a lone island in the stormy sea of imperialist robbery. The main economic factor in the West is that this imperialist war which has tortured and exhausted mankind has given rise to such complicated, such acute, such involved conflicts that again and again, at every step, the question of war and peace, the solution of the question to the advantage of one or other grouping, hangs by a thread. We have lived through precisely such a situation in the past few days. The contradictions that have arisen out of the frenzied struggle between the imperialist powers drawn into a war which is the result of the economic conditions of the development of capitalism over a number of decades, have made it impossible for the imperialists themselves to stop this war.

Owing to these contradictions, it has come about that the general alliance of the imperialists of all countries, forming the basis of the economic alliance of capitalism, an alliance whose natural and inevitable aim is to defend capital, which recognises no fatherland, and which has proved in the course of many major and important episodes in world history that capital places the safeguarding of the alliance of the capitalists of all countries against the working people above the interests of the fatherland, of the people or of what you will—that this alliance is not the moving force of politics.

Of course, as before, this alliance remains the main economic trend of the capitalist system, a trend which must ultimately make itself felt with inevitable force. That the imperialist war has divided into hostile groups, into hostile coalitions the imperialist powers which at the present moment, one may say, have divided up the whole world among themselves, is an exception to this main tendency of capitalism. This enmity, this struggle, this death grapple, proves that in certain circumstances the alliance of world imperialism is impossible. We are witnessing a situation in which the stormy waves of imperialist reaction, of the imperialist slaughter of nations, are hurling themselves at the small island of the socialist Soviet Republic, and seem about to sink it any minute, while actually these waves are only breaking against each other.

The basic contradictions between the imperialist powers have led to such a merciless struggle that, while recognising its hopelessness, neither the one, nor the other group is in a position to extricate itself at will from the iron grip of this war. The war has brought out two main contradictions, which in their turn have determined the socialist Soviet Republic's present international position. The first is the battle being waged on the Western front between Germany and Britain, which has reached an extreme degree of ferocity. We have heard on more than one occasion representatives of the two belligerent groups promise and assure their own people and other peoples that all that is required is one more last effort for the enemy to be subdued, the fatherland defended and the interests of civilisation and of the war of liberation saved for all time. The longer this terrible struggle drags on and the deeper the belligerent countries become involved, the further off is the way out of this interminable war. And it is the violence of this conflict that makes extremely difficult, well-nigh impossible, an alliance of the great imperialist powers against the Soviet Republic, which in the bare half-year of Its existence has won the warm regard and the most whole-hearted sympathy of the class-conscious workers of the world.

The second contradiction determining Russia's international position is the rivalry between Japan and America. Over several decades the economic development of these countries has produced a vast amount of inflammable material which makes inevitable a desperate clash between them for domination of the Pacific Ocean and the surrounding territories. The entire diplomatic and economic history of the Far East leaves no room for doubt that under capitalist conditions it is impossible to avert the imminent conflict between Japan and America. This contradiction, temporarily concealed by the alliance of Japan and America against Germany, delays Japanese imperialism's attack on Russia, which was prepared for over a long period, which was a long time feeling its way, and which to a certain degree was started and is being supported by counter-revolutionary forces. The campaign which has been launched against the Soviet Republic (the landing at Vladivostok and the support of the Semyonov bands) is being held up because it threatens to turn the hidden conflict between Japan and America into open war. It is quite likely, of course, and we must not forget that no matter how solid the imperialist groupings may appear to be, they can be broken up in a few days if the interests of sacred private property, the sacred rights of concessions, etc., demand it. It may well be that the tiniest spark will suffice to blow up the existing alignment of powers, and then the afore-mentioned contradictions will no longer protect us.

At the moment, however, the situation we have described explains why it is possible to preserve our socialist island in the middle of stormy seas and also why its position is so unstable, and, at times, to the great joy of the bourgeoisie and the panic of the petty bourgeoisie, it seems that it may be engulfed by the waves at any minute.

The outer aspect, the external expression of this situation is the Brest Treaty on the one hand, and the customs and laws with regard to neutral countries on the other.

You know that treaties and laws are worth nothing but a scrap of paper in the face of international conflicts.

These words are usually recalled and quoted as an example of the cynicism of imperialist foreign policy; the cynicism, however, lies not in these words, but in the ruthless, the cruelly and agonisingly ruthless, imperialist war, in which all peace treaties and all laws of neutrality have been flouted, are flouted, and will be flouted, as long as capitalism exists.

That is why, when we come to the most important question for us, the Brest peace and the likelihood of its violation with all the possible consequences for us — if we want to stand firmly on our socialist feet and do not want to be overthrown by the plots and provocations of the counter-revolutionaries, no matter under what socialist labels they disguise themselves, we must not forget for a single moment the economic principles underlying all peace treaties, including that of Brest-Litovsk, the economic principles underlying all neutrality, including our own. We must not forget, on the one hand, the state of affairs internationally, the state of affairs of international imperialism in relation to the class, which is growing, and which sooner or later, perhaps even later than we desire or expect, will nevertheless become capitalism's heir and will defeat world capitalism. And on the other hand, we must not forget the relations between the imperialist countries, the relations between the imperialist economic groups.

Having clarified this situation, I think, comrades, we shall not find it difficult to understand the significance of those diplomatic particulars and details, at times even trifles, which have mainly occupied our attention during the past few days, which have been on our minds during the past few days. Clearly, the instability of the international situation gives rise to panic. This panic emanates from the Constitutional-Democrats, the Right Socialist-Revolutionaries and Mensheviks, who aid and abet the interests of those who want and who strive to sow panic. In no way closing our eyes to the full danger and tragedy of the situation, and analysing the economic relations on an international scale, we must say: yes, the question of war and peace hangs by a thread both in the West and in the Far East because two trends exist; one, which makes an alliance of all the imperialists inevitable; the other, which places the imperialists in opposition to each other—two trends, neither of which has any firm foundation. No, Japan cannot now decide to launch a full-scale attack, although with her million-strong army she could quite easily overrun obviously weak Russia. I do not know, nor can anyone know, when this is likely to take place.

The form of the ultimatum threatens war against the allies and a treaty with Germany, but this position can change in a few days. There is always the possibility of it changing, because the American bourgeoisie, now at logger-heads with Japan, can tomorrow come to terms with her, because the Japanese bourgeoisie are just as likely tomorrow to come to terms with the German bourgeoisie. Their basic interests are the same: the division of the world between themselves, the interests of the landowners, of capital the safeguarding (as they say) of their national self-respect and their national interests. This language is sufficiently familiar to those who have either the misfortune or the habit—I don't know which—of reading newspapers like those of the Socialist-Revolutionaries. And when national self-respect begins to be mentioned frequently we all know, we know very well from the experience of 1914, what facts of imperialist robbery this is prompted by. In view of this relationship it is clear why the situation in the Far East is unstable. One thing must be said: we must have a clear understanding of these contradictions of capitalist interests, we must appreciate that the stability of the Soviet Republic is growing with every week, every month that passes, and that sympathy towards it among the working and exploited people of the world is growing at the same time.

And, at the same time, any day, any moment we must be prepared for and expect changes in international politics in favour of the policies of the extremist war parties.

The position of the German coalition is clear to us. At the present moment the majority of the German bourgeois parties stand for observing the Brest peace, but, of course, are very glad to "improve" on it and to receive a few more annexations at Russia's expense. What makes them take this stand? The political and military considerations of German national interests—as they express it—of imperialist interests, make them prefer peace in the East, so that their hands may be free in the West, where German imperialism has promised an immediate victory on many occasions, and where every week or every month proves that this victory, the more the partial successes gained, recedes still further into the distance. On the other hand, there is a war party which, during discussions on the Brest Treaty, showed its hand on a number of occasions, a party which naturally exists in all imperialist countries, a war party which says to itself: force must be used immediately, irrespective of possible consequences. These are the voices of the extremist war party. It has been known in German history since the time when overwhelming military victories became a feature history. It has been known since 1866, for instance, when the extremist war party of Germany achieved victory over Austria and turned this victory into a complete rout. All these clashes, all these conflicts are inevitable and lead to a situation where matters now hang by a thread, where, on the one hand, the bourgeois imperialist majority of the German parliament, the German propertied classes, the German capitalists prefer to stand by the Brest Treaty, while having, I repeat, no hesitation about improving on it. And on the other hand, any day, any moment we must be prepared for and expect changes in politics in the interests of the extremist war party.

This explains the instability of the international situation; this explains how easy it is in the circumstances to put the Party in one situation or another; this shows what prudence, caution, self-control and presence of mind is demanded of the Soviet government if it is to define its task clearly. Let the Russian bourgeoisie rush from a French to a German orientation. They like doing this. They have in several areas seen that German support is an excel lent guarantee against the peasants who are taking the land, and against the workers who are building the foundations of socialism. In the quite recent past, and over a long period, over a number of years they branded as traitors those who condemned the imperialist war and opened people's eyes to its real nature, but now they are all prepared in a few weeks to change their political beliefs and to go over from an alliance with the British robbers to an alliance with the German robbers against Soviet power. Let the bourgeoisie of all shades, from the Right Socialist-Revolutionaries and Mensheviks to the Left Socialist-Revolutionaries, rush this way and that. It suits their nature. Let them spread panic, for they are themselves in a panic. Let them rush to and from, unable to do otherwise, vacillating between the different orientations and between the absurd phrases that fail to take into consideration the fact that to deepen the effect of the revolution, when it has attained great proportions, one has to experience the most diverse groupings and transitions from one stage to another. We Russian revolutionaries have had the good fortune in the twentieth century to pass through two revolutions, each of which gave us a lot of experience, which has also stamped its impression on the lives of the people, of how a deep-going and effective revolutionary movement is prepared; how the different classes in this movement behave; by what difficult and exhausting path, sometimes by a long evolution, the maturity of new- classes comes about.

Remember how hard it was for the Soviets, created by the spontaneous outburst in 1905, how hard it was for them in 1917 to take up the fight again, and how hard later, when they had to go through all the suffering of compromise with the bourgeoisie and with the hidden, most rabid enemies of the working class, who talked of the defence of the revolution, of the Red Flag, and committed the greatest of crimes in June 1917—now, when the majority of the working class supports us, remember what it cost after the great 1905 Revolution to emerge with Soviets of the working and peasant classes. Remember all this, and think of the mass scale on which the struggle against international imperialism is developing, think how difficult the transition to this situation is, and what the Russian Republic had to undergo when it found itself ahead of all the other contingents of the socialist army.

I know that there are, of course, wiseacres with a high opinion of themselves and even calling themselves socialists, who assert that power should not have been taken until the revolution broke out **in all countries.** They do not realise that in saying this they are deserting the revolution and going over to the side of the bourgeoisie. **To wait until the working classes carry out a revolution on an international scale means** that everyone will remain suspended in mid-air. This is senseless. Everyone knows the difficulties of a revolution. It may begin with brilliant success in one country and then go through agonising periods, since final victory is only possible on a world scale, and only by the joint efforts of the workers of all countries. Our task consists in being restrained and prudent, we must manoeuvre and retreat until we receive reinforcements. A change over to these tactics is inevitable, no matter how much they are mocked by so-called revolutionaries with no idea of what revolution means.

Having dealt with the general questions I now want to examine the causes of the recent alarm and panic which have again enabled the counter-revolutionaries to start activities intended to undermine Soviet power.

I have already mentioned that the outward legal form and outer aspect of all international relations of the Soviet Socialist Republic are, on the one hand, the Brest-Litovsk Treaty, and, on the other, the general law and custom defining the status of a neutral country among other, belligerent countries; this status accounts for the recent difficulties. The conclusion of peace with Finland, the Ukraine and Turkey should have been the natural consequence of the Brest-Litovsk Treaty, yet we are still at war with these countries, and this is not due to our internal development, but to the influence of the ruling classes of these countries. In these conditions the only temporary way out lay in the temporary breathing-space provided by the Brest-Litovsk Treaty, the breathing-space which provoked so many futile and unnecessary words about its being impossible but which nevertheless turned out to be possible and in two months brought results, made itself felt on the majority of Russian soldiers, enabled them to return home and see how things were going, to take advantage of the revolution's gains, to work the land, to look around and draw new strength for the fresh sacrifices ahead.

Naturally, this temporary breathing-space appeared to be coming to an end when the situation worsened in Finland, the Ukraine and Turkey, when, instead of peace, we merely obtained a postponement of that selfsame acute economic problem: war or peace? And now are we to go to war once again, despite all the peaceful intentions of Soviet power and its absolute determination to sacrifice so-called Great Power status, i.e., the right to conclude secret treaties, to conceal them from the people with the assistance of the Chernovs, Tseretelis and Kerenskys, to sign secret predatory treaties and conduct an imperialist, predatory war? Indeed, instead of peace, all that we have obtained is a brief postponement of that selfsame pressing question of war or peace.

Here is the result of this situation, and you again clearly see where its final outcome lies—namely, in the question of what the results will be of the wavering among the two hostile groups of imperialist countries—the American conflict in the Far East, and the German-British conflict in Western Europe. It is clear how these contradictions have intensified over the conquest of the Ukraine, over the situation which the German imperialists, particularly their main war party, frequently viewed so optimistically looked upon as so easy, and which caused precisely this extremist German war party such fantastic difficulties. It was this situation which temporarily raised the hopes of the Russian Constitutional-Democrats, Mensheviks and Right Socialist-Revolutionaries, who have fallen in love with what Skoropadsky is bringing the Ukraine, and who now hope that this will also be easily achieved in Russia. These gentlemen will be mistaken; their hopes will turn to dust because. . . (stormy applause), because, I say, that same main war party in Germany, which is too accustomed to rely on the power of the sword, even this party in these particular circumstances has not been supported by the majority of the imperialists, those bourgeois imperialist circles who have seen unprecedented difficulties in the conquest of the Ukraine, in the struggle to subjugate a whole people, in the forced necessity of resorting to a terrible coup d'etat.

This main war party created unprecedented difficulties in Germany when, having promised its people and the workers supreme victories on the Western Front, this extremist war party was forced to recognise that it was faced with new, unbelievable economic and political difficulties with having to divert military forces to tasks which also at first seemed easy, and also with having to conclude a treaty with the Ukrainian Mensheviks and the Right Socialist-Revolutionaries, who were the signatories to the peace treaty.

The extremist war party in Germany reasoned: we shall send many troops and obtain grain, but then it became necessary to engineer a coup d'etat. That turned out to be easy, because the Ukrainian Mensheviks readily supported this move. But it then turned out that this coup d'etat created fresh and gigantic difficulties, because the grain and raw materials, without which Germany cannot exist, had to be fought for at every step, and their appropriation by military force in an occupied country involved too great an effort and too many sacrifices.

Such is the situation that has arisen in the Ukraine and that should have lent wings to the hopes of the Russian counter-revolution. It is clear that in this struggle, Russia, which has been unable to rebuild her army, has suffered and is suffering further losses. The peace talks have led to new, onerous conditions, to new open and concealed indemnities. Under what decree the Ukraine's frontiers are to be determined is not clear. The Rada, [2] which signed the decree, has been removed. A landowner-hetman has been put in its place. Because of this uncertainty a whole number of problems have emerged which prove that the questions of war and peace remain as before. The partial armistice existing between the Russian and German troops in no way predetermines the general situation. The question hangs in the air. The same is true of Georgia, where we have a protracted counter-revolutionary struggle by the government of the Caucasian Mensheviks, a protracted struggle by counter-revolutionaries who call themselves Social-Democrats. And when the victory of Soviet power and the working people, having embraced the whole of Russia, has begun to draw in the non-Russian outlying areas, when it has become quite obvious and beyond all doubt that the victory of Soviet power, as has been admitted by the counter-revolutionary representatives of the Don Cossacks, cannot be delayed, when the Menshevik government in the Caucasus has begun to waver the government of Gegechkori and Jordania, who realised this too late and started to talk about finding a common language with the Bolsheviks when Tsereteli, aided by the Turkish troops, has shown his hand by advancing against the Bolsheviks—they will reap the same harvest as the Rada. (Applause.)

Remember, however, that if these bargainers of the Caucasian Rada receive the support of the German troops, as did the Ukrainian Rada, then there will no doubt be fresh difficulties for the Russian Soviet Republic, a new inevitability of war, new dangers and now uncertainties. There are people who refer to this uncertainty, to the strain of an uncertain situation (in fact such an uncertain situation is sometimes worse than any clearly defined one), and say that the uncertainty can be easily removed—you only have to demand openly that the Germans observe the Brest Treaty.

I have heard such naïve people, who consider themselves to be on the left, but who in fact only reflect the narrow mindedness of our petty bourgeoisie. . . .

They forget that you have first to be victorious before you can make demands. If you are not victorious the enemy can delay his reply or even make no reply at all to your demands. That is the law of imperialist war.

You don't like it. Then be able to defend your homeland. The worker has every right to defend his homeland for the sake of socialism, for the sake of the working class.

I shall only add that this uncertain situation on the Caucasian border was a result of the quite unpardonable vacillation of the Gegechkori government which at first announced that it did not recognise the Brest peace, and then declared its independence without informing us of what territory this independence covered. We have sent innumerable radio-telegrams saying to them, please inform us of the territory you lay claim to. You have the right to claim independence, but since you speak of independence, you are bound to say what territory you are representing. That was a week ago. Countless radio-telegrams have been dispatched, but not a single reply has been received. German imperialism is taking advantage of this. This has made it possible for Germany, and Turkey, as a satellite state, to push farther and farther forward, making no replies, ignoring everything, stating: we shall take whatever we can, we are not infringing the Brest peace, because the Transcaucasian army does not recognise it, because the Caucasus is independent.

Of whom is the Gegechkori government independent? It is independent of the Soviet Republic, but it is dependent, just a little, on German imperialism, and quite naturally so. (Applause.)

That is the situation which has developed, comrades—an acute aggravation of relations in the last few days—it is a situation which has once again, and fairly obviously, confirmed the correctness of the tactics which the vast majority of our Party, the Russian Communist Party of Bolsheviks, has employed and firmly insisted on during recent months.

We possess great revolutionary experience, which has taught us that it is essential to employ the tactics of merciless attack when objective conditions permit, when the experience of compromising has shown that the people's indignation has been aroused, and that attack will express this change. But we have to resort to temporising tactics, to a slow gathering of forces when objective circumstances do not favour a call for a general merciless repulse.

Any person who does not shut his eyes to the facts, who is not blind, knows that we are merely repeating what we have said earlier, and what we have always said: that we do not forget the weakness of the Russian working class compared to other contingents of the international proletariat. It was not our own will, but historical circumstances, the legacy of the tsarist regime, the flabbiness of the Russian bourgeoisie, that caused this contingent to march ahead of the other contingents of the international proletariat; it was not because we desired it, but because circumstances demanded it. We must remain at our post until the arrival of our ally, the international proletariat, which will arrive and will inevitably arrive, but which is approaching at an immeasurably slower pace than we expect or wish. If we see that as a result of objective conditions the international proletariat moves too slowly, we must nevertheless stick to our tactics of temporising and utilising the conflicts and contradictions between the imperialists, of slowly accumulating strength; the tactics of preserving this island of Soviet power in the stormy imperialist sea, maintaining this island which now already attracts the gaze of the working people of all countries. That is why we tell ourselves that, if the extremist war party can at any moment defeat any imperialist coalition and build a new unexpected imperialist coalition against us, we at any rate will not make it any easier for them. And if they come against us—yes, we are now defencists—we shall do everything in our power, everything within the power of diplomatic tactics, we shall do everything to delay that moment, everything to make the brief and unstable respite, given us in March, last longer, for we are firmly convinced that behind us are tens of millions of workers and peasants who know that with every week and, even more so, with every month of this respite they gain new strength, they are consolidating Soviet power, making it firm and stable. They know that they are introducing a new spirit, and that after the attrition and weariness of this exhausting reactionary war, they will create firmness and readiness for the last and decisive battle should external forces attack the Socialist Soviet Republic.

We have been defencists since October 25, 1917; we have won the right to defend our native land. It is not secret treaties that we are defending, we have annulled and exposed them to the whole world. We are defending our country against the imperialists. We are defending and we shall win. It is not the Great Power status of Russia that we are defending—of that nothing is left but Russia proper—nor is it national interests, for we assert that the interests of socialism, of world socialism are higher than national interests, higher than the interests of the state. We are defenders of the socialist fatherland.

This is not achieved by issuing declarations, but only by overthrowing the bourgeoisie in one's own country, by a ruthless war to the death begun in one's own country; and we know that we shall win this war. Ours is a small island in the war that engulfs the imperialist world, but on this small island we have shown and proved to all what the working class can do. Everyone knows this and has acknowledged it. We have proved that we possess the right to defend our homeland. We are defencists and look upon our task with all the seriousness taught us by the four years of war, with all the seriousness and caution understood by every worker and peasant who has met a soldier and has learned what that soldier has lived through in these four years of war—the caution which may not be understood, which may be sneered at and regarded frivolously only by people who are revolutionaries in word but not in deed. It is just because we do support the defence of the fatherland that we tell ourselves: a firm and strong army and a strong rear are needed for the defence, and in order to have a firm and strong army we must in the first place ensure that the food supplies are on a sound basis. For this the dictatorship of the proletariat must be expressed not only centrally—that is the first step and only the first step—but there must be dictatorship throughout the whole of Russia—that is the second step and only the second step, which we have not yet carried out sufficiently. Proletarian discipline is essential and necessary for us; real proletarian dictatorship, when the firm and iron rule of class-conscious workers is felt in every remote corner of our country, when not a single kulak, not a single rich man, not a single opponent of the grain monopoly remains unpunished, but is found and punished by the iron hand of the disciplined dictators of the working class, the proletarian dictators. (Applause.)

We say to ourselves: our attitude to defence of the fatherland is a cautious one; it is our duty to do everything that our diplomacy can do to delay the moment of war, to extend the respite period; we promise the workers and peasants to do all we can for peace. This we shall do. And bourgeois gentlemen and their hirelings, who think that just as in the Ukraine, where a coup was brought about so easily, so in Russia it may be possible to give birth to new Skoropadskys, should not forget that the war party in Germany found it very difficult to effect a coup in the Ukraine, and will meet with plenty of opposition in Soviet Russia. Everything goes to prove this; Soviet power has pursued this line and has made every sacrifice to consolidate the position of the working people.

The situation with regard to peace with Finland may be summed up in the words: Fort Ino and Murmansk. Fort Ino, which defends Petrograd, lies geographically within the Finnish state. In concluding peace with the workers' government of Finland we, the representatives of socialist Russia, recognised Finland's absolute right to the whole territory, but it was mutually agreed by both governments that Fort Ino should remain in Russia's hands "for the defence of the joint interests of the Socialist Republics", as stated in the treaty that was concluded. [3] It is natural that our troops should conclude this peace in Finland, should sign these terms. It is natural that bourgeois and counter-revolutionary Finland was bound to raise a hue and cry against this. It is natural that the reactionary and counter-revolutionary Finnish bourgeoisie should lay claim to this stronghold. It is natural that, because of this, the issue should become acute on a number of occasions and should still remain acute. Matters hang by a thread. It is natural that the question of Murmansk, to which the Anglo-French have laid claim, should give rise to even greater aggravation, because they have spent tens of millions on the port's construction in order to safeguard their military rear in their imperialist war against Germany. Their respect for neutrality is so wonderful that they make use of everything that is left unguarded. Furthermore, sufficient excuse for their grabbing is their possession of a battleship, while we have nothing with which to chase it away. It is natural that all this should have aggravated the situation. There is an outer aspect, a legal expression resulting from the international position of the Soviet Republic, which presumes that it is impossible for armed forces of any belligerent state to set foot on neutral territory without being disarmed. The British landed their military forces at Murmansk, and we were unable to prevent this by armed force. Consequently, we are presented with demands almost in the nature of an ultimatum: if you cannot protect your neutrality, we shall wage war on your territory.

A worker-peasant army, however, has now been formed, it has rallied in the uyezds and gubernias the peasants who have returned to their land, land wrested from the landowners; they now have something to defend. An army has been formed which has started to build Soviet power, and which will become the vanguard if an invasion against Russia breaks out; we shall rise as one man to meet the enemy.

My time is up, and I want to conclude by reading a telegram received by radio from Comrade Joffe, Soviet Ambassador in Berlin. This telegram will show you that, on the one hand, you have confirmation from our Ambassador of whether my analysis of the international situation is correct and, on the other hand, that the foreign policy of our Soviet Republic is a responsible one—it is a policy of preparation for defence of our country, a steadfast policy, not allowing a single step to be taken that would aid the extremist parties of the imperialist powers in the East and West. This is a responsible policy with no illusions. There always remains the possibility that any day military forces may be thrown against us and we, the workers and peasants, assure ourselves and the whole world, and shall be able to prove, that we shall rise to a man to defend the Soviet Republic. I hope, therefore, that the reading of

82

this telegram will serve as an appropriate conclusion to my speech and will show us the spirit in which the representatives of the Soviet Republic work abroad in the interests of the Soviets, of all Soviet institutions and the Soviet Republic.

"The latest radio-telegrams received today report that the German War Prisoners' Commission is leaving on Friday, May 10. We have already received a Note from the German Government proposing the setting up of a special commission to consider all legal questions in regard to our possessions in the Ukraine and in Finland. I have agreed to such a commission and have asked you to send the appropriate military and legal representatives. Today I had a talk about further advances, demands for clearing Fort Ino, and the attitude of the Russians to Germany. Here is the reply: The German High Command states that there will be no further advances; Germany's role in the Ukraine and Finland has ended. Germany is willing to assist our peace talks with Kiev and Helsingfors and is entering into negotiations with the governments concerned. As regards Fort Ino, in connection with the Finnish Peace talks: according to the treaty, the forts should be destroyed. Germany considers that when defining the frontiers the agreement with the Reds can be accepted; the Whites have not yet replied. The German Government declares officially: Germany abides firmly by the Brest Treaty, she wants peaceful relations with us, she has no aggressive plans and has no intention of attacking us in any way. It is promised that, in accordance with my request, Russian citizens in Germany will be treated on a par with other neutrals."

The Higher Phase of Communist Society

The State & Revolution

August - September 1917
Source: Collected Works, Volume 25, p. 381-492

Marx continues:

"In a higher phase of communist society, after the enslaving subordination of the individual to the division of labor, and with it also the antithesis between mental and physical labor, has vanished, after labor has become not only a livelihood but life's prime want, after the productive forces have increased with the all-round development of the individual, and all the springs of co-operative wealth flow more abundantly--only then can the narrow horizon of bourgeois law be left behind in its entirety and society inscribe on its banners: From each according to his ability, to each according to his needs!"

Only now can we fully appreciate the correctness of Engels' remarks mercilessly ridiculing the absurdity of combining the words "freedom" and "state". So long as the state exists there is no freedom. When there is freedom, there will be no state.

The economic basis for the complete withering away of the state is such a high state of development of communism at which the antithesis between mental and physical labor disappears, at which there consequently disappears one of the principal sources of modern social inequality--a source, moreover, which cannot on any account be removed immediately by the mere conversion of the means of production into public property, by the mere expropriation of the capitalists.

This expropriation will make it possible for the productive forces to develop to a tremendous extent. And when we see how incredibly capitalism is already retarding this development, when we see how much progress could be achieved on the basis of the level of technique already attained, we are entitled to say with the fullest confidence that the expropriation of the capitalists will inevitably result in an enormous development of the productive forces of human society. But how rapidly this development will proceed, how soon it will reach the point of breaking away from the division of labor, of doing away with the antithesis between mental and physical labor, of transforming labor into "life's prime want"--we do not and cannot know.

That is why we are entitled to speak only of the inevitable withering away of the state, emphasizing the protracted nature of this process and its dependence upon the rapidity of development of the higher phase of communism, and leaving the question of the time required for, or the concrete forms of, the withering away quite open, because there is no material for answering these questions.

The state will be able to wither away completely when society adopts the rule: "From each according to his ability, to each according to his needs", i.e., when people have become so accustomed to observing the fundamental rules of social intercourse and when their labor has become so productive that they will voluntarily work according to their ability. "The narrow horizon of bourgeois law", which compels one to calculate with the heartlessness of a Shylock whether one has not worked half an hour more than anybody else--this narrow horizon will then be left behind. There will then be no need for society, in distributing the products, to regulate the quantity to be received by each; each will take freely "according to his needs".

From the bourgeois point of view, it is easy to declare that such a social order is "sheer utopia" and to sneer at the socialists for promising everyone the right to receive from society, without any control over the labor of the individual citizen, any quantity of truffles, cars, pianos, etc. Even to this day, most bourgeois "savants" confine themselves to sneering in this way, thereby betraying both their ignorance and their selfish defence of capitalism.

Ignorance--for it has never entered the head of any socialist to "promise" that the higher phase of the development of communism will arrive; as for the greatest socialists' forecast that it will arrive, it presupposes not the present ordinary run of people, who, like the seminary students in Pomyalovsky's stories,[2] are capable of damaging the stocks of public wealth "just for fun", and of demanding the impossible.

Until the "higher" phase of communism arrives, the socialists demand the strictest control by society and by the state over the measure of labor and the measure of consumption; but this control must start with the expropriation of the capitalists, with the establishment of workers' control over the capitalists, and must be exercised not by a state of bureaucrats, but by a state of armed workers.

The selfish defence of capitalism by the bourgeois ideologists (and their hangers-on, like the Tseretelis, Chernovs, and Co.) consists in that they substitute arguing and talk about the distant future for the vital and burning question of present-day politics, namely, the expropriation of the capitalists, the conversion of all citizens into workers and other employees of one huge "syndicate"--the whole state--and the complete subordination of the entire work of this syndicate to a genuinely democratic state, the state of the Soviets of Workers' and Soldiers' Deputies.

In fact, **when a learned professor, followed by the philistine,** followed in turn by the Tseretelis and Chernovs, **talks of wild utopias,** of the demagogic promises of the Bolsheviks, **of the impossibility of "introducing" socialism**, it is **the higher stage,** or **phase, of communism he has in mind,** which no one has ever promised or even thought to **"introduce", because, generally speaking, it cannot be "introduced".**

And this brings us to the question of the scientific distinction between socialism and communism which Engels touched on in his above-quoted argument about the incorrectness of the name "Social-Democrat". Politically, the distinction between the first, or lower, and the higher phase of communism will in time, probably, be tremendous. But it would be ridiculous to recognize this distinction now, under capitalism, and only individual anarchists, perhaps, could invest it with primary importance (if there still are people among the anarchists who have learned nothing from the "Plekhanov" conversion of the Kropotkins, of Grave, Corneliseen, and other "stars" of anarchism into social- chauvinists or "anarcho-trenchists", as Ghe, one of the few anarchists who have still preserved a sense of humor and a conscience, has put it).

But **the scientific distinction between socialism and communism is clear.** What is usually called socialism was termed by Marx the "first", or lower, phase of communist society. Insofar as the means of production becomes common property, the word "communism" is also applicable here, providing we do not forget that this is not complete communism. The great significance of Marx's explanations is that here, too, he consistently applies materialist dialectics, the theory of development, and regards communism as something which develops out of capitalism. Instead of scholastically invented, "concocted" definitions and fruitless disputes over words (What is socialism? What is communism?), Marx gives an analysis of what might be called the stages of the economic maturity of communism.

In its first phase, or first stage, communism cannot as yet be fully mature economically and entirely free from traditions or vestiges of capitalism. Hence the interesting phenomenon that communism in its first phase retains "the narrow horizon of bourgeois law". Of course, bourgeois law in regard to the distribution of consumer goods inevitably presupposes the existence of the bourgeois state, for law is nothing without an apparatus capable of enforcing the observance of the rules of law.

It follows that under communism there remains for a time not only bourgeois law, but even the bourgeois state, without the bourgeoisie!

This may sound like a paradox or simply a dialectical conundrum of which Marxism is often accused by people who have not taken the slightest trouble to study its extraordinarily profound content.

But in fact, remnants of the old, surviving in the new, confront us in life at every step, both in nature and in society. And Marx did not arbitrarily insert a scrap of "bourgeois" law into communism, but indicated what is economically and politically inevitable in a society emerging out of the womb of capitalism.

Democracy means equality. The great significance of the proletariat's struggle for equality and of equality as a slogan will be clear if we correctly interpret it as meaning the abolition of classes. But democracy means only formal equality. And as soon as equality is achieved for all members of society in relation to ownership of the means of production, that is, equality of labor and wages, humanity will inevitably be confronted with the question of advancing further from formal equality to actual equality, i.e., to the operation of the rule "from each according to his ability, to each according to his needs". By what stages, by means of what practical measures humanity will proceed to this supreme aim we do not and cannot know. But it is important to realize how infinitely mendacious is the ordinary bourgeois conception of socialism as something lifeless, rigid, fixed once and for all, whereas in reality only socialism will be the beginning of a rapid, genuine, truly mass forward movement, embracing first the majority and then the whole of the population, in all spheres of public and private life.

Democracy is of enormous importance to the working class in its struggle against the capitalists for its emancipation. But democracy is by no means a boundary not to be overstepped; it is only one of the stages on the road from feudalism to capitalism, and from capitalism to communism.

Democracy is a form of the state, it represents, on the one hand, the organized, systematic use of force against persons; but, on the other hand, it signifies the formal recognition of equality of citizens, the equal right of all to determine the structure of, and to administer, the state. This, in turn, results in the fact that, at a certain stage in the development of democracy, it first welds together the class that wages a revolutionary struggle against capitalism--the proletariat, and enables it to crush, smash to atoms, wipe off the face of the earth the bourgeois, even the republican-bourgeois, state machine, the standing army, the police and the bureaucracy and to substitute for them a more democratic state machine, but a state machine nevertheless, in the shape of armed workers who proceed to form a militia involving the entire population.

Here "quantity turns into quality": such a degree of democracy implies overstepping the boundaries of bourgeois society and beginning its socialist reorganization. If really all take part in the administration of the state, capitalism cannot retain its hold. The development of capitalism, in turn, creates the preconditions that enable really "all" to take part in the administration of the state. Some of these preconditions are: universal literacy, which has already been achieved in a number of the most advanced capitalist countries, then the "training and disciplining" of millions of workers by the huge, complex, socialized apparatus of the postal service, railways, big factories, large-scale commerce, banking, etc., etc.

Given these economic preconditions, it is quite possible, after the overthrow of the capitalists and the bureaucrats, to proceed immediately, overnight, to replace them in the control over production and distribution, in the work of keeping account of labor and products, by the armed workers, by the whole of the armed population. (The question of control and accounting should not be confused with the question of the scientifically trained staff of engineers, agronomists, and so on. These gentlemen are working today in obedience to the wishes of the capitalists and will work even better tomorrow in obedience to the wishes of the armed workers.)

Accounting and control--that is mainly what is needed for the "smooth working", for the proper functioning, of the first phase of communist society. All citizens are transformed into hired employees of the state, which consists of the armed workers. All citizens become employees and workers of a single countrywide state "syndicate". All that is required is that they should work equally, do their proper share of work, and get equal pay; the accounting and control necessary for this have been simplified by capitalism to the utmost and reduced to the extraordinarily simple operations--which any literate person can perform--of supervising and recording, knowledge of the four rules of arithmetic, and issuing appropriate receipts.

When the majority of the people begin independently and everywhere to keep such accounts and exercise such control over the capitalists (now converted into employees) and over the intellectual gentry who preserve their capitalist habits, this control will really become universal, general, and popular; and there will be no getting away from it, there will be "nowhere to go".

The whole of society will have become a single office and a single factory, with equality of labor and pay.

But this "factory" discipline, which the proletariat, after defeating the capitalists, after overthrowing the exploiters, will extend to the whole of society, is by no means our ideal, or our ultimate goal. It is only a necessary step for thoroughly cleansing society of all the infamies and abominations of capitalist exploitation, and for further progress.

From the moment all members of society, or at least the vast majority, have learned to administer the state themselves, have taken this work into their own hands, have organized control over the insignificant capitalist minority, over the gentry who wish to preserve their capitalist habits and over the workers who have been thoroughly corrupted by capitalism--from this moment the need for government of any kind begins to disappear altogether. The more complete the democracy, the nearer the moment when it becomes unnecessary. The more democratic the "state" which consists of the armed workers, and which is "no longer a state in the proper sense of the word", the more rapidly every form of state begins to wither away.

For when all have learned to administer and actually to independently administer social production, independently keep accounts and exercise control over the parasites, the sons of the wealthy, the swindlers and other "guardians of capitalist traditions", the escape from this popular accounting and control will inevitably become so incredibly difficult, such a rare exception, and will probably be accompanied by such swift and severe punishment (for the armed workers are practical men and not sentimental intellectuals, and they scarcely allow anyone to trifle with them), that the necessity of observing the simple, fundamental rules of the community will very soon become a habit.

Then the door will be thrown wide open for the transition from the first phase of communist society to its higher phase, and with it to the complete withering away of the state.

First All-Russia Congress on Adult Education

May 6-19, 1919
Lenin Collected Works, Volume 29, pages 333-376

I shall now pass from freedom to equality. This is a much more profound subject. This brings us to a still more serious, a more painful question, one that gives rise to considerable disagreement.

The revolution in its course sweeps away one exploiting class after another. First, it swept away the monarchy, and by equality implied an elected government, a republic. Proceeding further it swept away the landowners; and you know that the keynote of the entire struggle against the medieval system, against feudalism, was the slogan "equality". All are equal irrespective of social-estate; all are equal, millionaires and paupers alike. This is what the great revolutionaries of the period that has gone into history as the period of the great French Revolution said, thought and sincerely believed. The slogan of the revolution against the landowners was equality, and by equality was meant that the millionaires and the workers should have equal rights. The revolution developed. It said that "equality" — we did not specify this in our programme, for one cannot go on repeating the same thing endlessly; it is as clear as what we said about freedom — that equality is a deception if it runs counter to the emancipation of labour from the yoke of capital. That is what we say, and it is absolutely true. We say that a democratic republic with present-day equality is a fraud, a deception; here there is no equality, nor can there be. It is prevented by the private ownership of the means of production and money, capital. It is possible, at one stroke, to confiscate privately owned mansions and fine buildings, it is possible in a relatively short period to confiscate capital and the means of production. But try to abolish the private ownership of money.

Money is congealed social wealth, congealed social labour. Money is a token which enables its owner to take tribute from all the working people. Money is a survival of yesterday's exploitation.

That is what money is. Can it be abolished at one stroke? No. Even before the socialist revolution the socialists wrote that it is impossible to abolish money at one stroke, and our experience corroborates this. There must be very considerable technical and, what is much more difficult and much more important, organisational achievement before we can abolish money; and until then we must put up with equality in words, in the constitution; we must put up with a situation in which everybody who possesses money practically has the right to exploit. We could not abolish money at one stroke. We say that for the time being money will remain and remain for a fairly long time in the transition period from the old capitalist system to the new socialist system. Equality is a deception if it runs counter to the emancipation of labour from the yoke of capital.

Engels was a thousand times right when he said that the concept of equality is a most absurd and stupid prejudice if it does not imply the abolition of classes.[4] Bourgeois professors attempted to use the concept equality as grounds for accusing us of wanting all men to be alike. They themselves invented this absurdity and wanted to ascribe it to the socialists. But in their ignorance, they did not know that the socialists—and precisely the founders of modern scientific socialism, Marx and Engels—had said: equality is an empty phrase if it does not imply the abolition of classes. We want to abolish classes, and in this sense we are for equality. But the claim that we want all men to be alike is just nonsense, the silly invention of an intellectual who sometimes conscientiously strikes a pose, juggles with words, but says nothing—I don't care whether he calls himself a writer, a scholar, or anything else.

But we say that our goal is equality, and **by that we mean the abolition of classes.** Then the class distinction between workers and peasants should be abolished. That is exactly our object. **A society in which the class distinction between workers and peasants still exists is neither a communist society nor a socialist society.** True, if the word socialism is interpreted in a certain sense, **it might be called a socialist society,** but that would be mere sophistry, an argument about words. **Socialism is the first stage of communism**; but it is not worthwhile arguing about words. One thing is clear, and that is, that **as long as the class distinction between workers and peasants exists, it is no use talking about equality,** unless we want to bring grist to the mill of the bourgeoisie. The peasantry constitute a class of the patriarchal era, a class which has been reared by decades and centuries of slavery; and throughout all these decades the peasants existed as small proprietors, first, under the heel of other classes, and later, formally free and equal, but as property-owners and the owners of food products.

This brings us to the question which most of all rouses the ire of our enemies, which most of all creates doubt in the minds of inexperienced and thoughtless people, and which separates us most of all from those would-be democrats and socialists who are offended because we do not recognise them as such, but call them supporters of the capitalists, perhaps due to their ignorance, but supporters of the capitalists all the same.

Their social conditions, production, living and economic conditions make the peasant half worker and half huckster.

This is a fact. And you cannot get away from this fact until you have abolished money, until you have abolished exchange. And for this years and years of the stable rule by the proletariat is needed; for only the proletariat is capable of vanquishing the bourgeoisie. We are told: "You are violators of equality, you have violated equality not only with the exploiters—'with this I am inclined to agree', some Socialist-Revolutionary or Menshevik who does not know what he is talking about may say—but you have violated equality between the workers and the peasants, you have violated the equality of 'labour democracy', you are criminals!" In answer to this we say: "Yes, we have violated equality between the workers and peasants, and we assert that you who stand for this equality are supporters of Kolchak." Recently I read a splendid article by Comrade Germanov, in Pravda, in which he deals with the theses drawn up by Citizen Sher, one of the most "socialistic" of the Menshevik Social-Democrats. These theses were submitted to one of our co-operative organisations, and they are of such a nature that they deserve to be engraved on a tablet and hung up in every volost executive committee with an inscription underneath stating: "This is Kolchak's man."

I know perfectly well that Citizen Sher and his friends will call me a slanderer for this, and perhaps something worse. Nevertheless, I invite those people who have learned the ABC of political economy and of politics to make a very careful study to see who is right and who is wrong. Citizen Sher says that the Soviet government's food policy, and its economic policy in general, is all wrong; that it is necessary, gradually at first, and then to an increasing degree, to grant freedom to trade in food products, and to safeguard private property.

I say that this is Kolchak's economic programme, his economic basis. I assert that anybody who has read Marx, especially the first chapter of Capital, anybody who has read at least Kautsky's popular outline of Marx's theories entitled The Economic Theories of Karl Marx, must come to the conclusion that in the midst of a proletarian revolution against the bourgeoisie, at a time when landowner and capitalist property is being abolished, when the country that has been ruined by four years of imperialist war is starving, freedom to trade in grain would mean freedom for the capitalists, freedom to restore the rule of capital. This is Kolchak's economic programme, for Kolchak does not rest on air.

It is rather silly to denounce Kolchak only because of the atrocities he committed against the workers, or even because he flogged schoolmistresses for sympathising with the Bolsheviks. This is a vulgar defence of democracy, a silly accusation against Kolchak. Kolchak operates with the means he has at hand. But what is his economic basis? His basis is freedom of trade. This is what he stands for; and this is why all the capitalists support him. But you say: "I have left Kolchak; I do not support him." This stands to your credit, of course; but it does not prove that you have a head on your shoulders and are able to think. This is the answer we give to these people, without casting any slur on the honour of the Socialist-Revolutionaries and the Mensheviks who deserted Kolchak when they realised that he is a tyrant. But if such people, in a country which is fighting a desperate struggle against Kolchak, continue to fight for the "equality of labour democracy", for freedom to trade in grain, they are still supporting Kolchak, the only trouble being that they do not understand this and cannot reason logically.

Kolchak—it does not matter whether his name is Kolchak or Denikin, their uniforms may be different, but their natures are the same—is able to hold out because, having captured a region rich in grain, he grants freedom to trade in grain and permits the free restoration of capitalism. This was the case in all revolutions, and this will be the case in this country if we abandon the dictatorship of the proletariat for the sake of the "freedom" and "equality" of the democratic, Socialist-Revolutionary, Left Menshevik and other gentlemen, sometimes including the anarchists—the number of titles is infinite. In the Ukraine at the present time, every gang chooses a political title, each more free and democratic than the other, and there is a gang to every uyezd.

The "advocates of the interests of the working peasantry", mainly the Socialist-Revolutionaries, propose equality between the workers and the peasants. Others, like Citizen Sher, have studied Marxism, but they still do not understand that there can be no equality between the workers and the peasants in the period of transition from capitalism to socialism, and that those who promise this should be regarded as advocating Kolchak's programme, even if they do so unwittingly. I assert that anybody who gives some thought to the actual conditions prevailing in this completely ruined country will understand this.

The "socialists" who assert that in this country we are in the period of the bourgeois revolution, constantly accuse us of having introduced "consumers'" communism. Some of them say it is communism for soldiers, and imagine that they are superior to this, imagine that they have risen above this "base" form of communism. **But these are simply people who juggle with words.** They have seen books, studied hooks, repeat what is in books, but they understand nothing about what the books say. There are scholars, and even very learned scholars, like that. They have read in books that socialism represents the highest development of production. Kautsky does nothing else but repeat this sort of thing even now. The other day I read in a German newspaper, which got here by accident, a report of the last Congress of Workers' Councils in Germany. Kautsky was one of the rapporteurs at this Congress, and in his report he emphasised—not he personally, but his wife; he was sick, and so his wife read the report—in this report he emphasised that socialism represents the highest development of production, that without production neither capitalism nor socialism was possible, and that this the German workers did not understand.

Poor German workers. They are fighting Scheidemann and Noske, fighting against the butchers, striving to overthrow the power of Scheidemann and Noske, the butchers who continue to call themselves Social-Democrats, and they think civil war is going on! Liebknecht was murdered, and so was Rosa Luxemburg. All the Russian bourgeois say—and this was stated in an Ekaterinodar newspaper: "This is what ought to be done to our Bolsheviks!" This is exactly what this paper stated. Those who understand what is going on know perfectly well that this is the opinion of the entire world bourgeoisie. We must defend ourselves. Scheidemann and Noske are waging civil war against the proletariat. War is war. The German workers think that they are in a state of civil war and all other questions are of minor importance. The first task is to feed the workers. Kautsky thinks that this is "soldiers'" or "consumers'" communism, and that it is necessary to develop production! . . .

Oh, how clever you are, gentlemen! But how can production be developed in a country that is being plundered and ruined by the imperialists, and which lacks coal, raw materials and machinery?

"Develop production!" There is not a meeting of the Council of People's Commissars, or of the Council of Defence that does not share out the last millions of poods of coal or oil, and find ourselves in a terrible fix when the commissars take the last scraps and even then no one has enough, and we have to decide which factory to close down, in which place to leave the workers without work—a painful question, but one we are compelled to decide because we have no coal. The coal is in the Donets Basin; the coal has been destroyed by the German invaders. This is a typical state of affairs. Take Belgium or Poland. The same thing is happening everywhere as a consequence of the imperialist war. Hence, unemployment and starvation are likely to last many years, for some flooded mines take many years to restore. And yet we are told that socialism means increasing output. You have read books, good, kind gentlemen, you have written books, but you don't understand a scrap of what is in the books. (Applause.)

Of course, if it were a case of capitalist society in peace time, peacefully developing into socialism, there would be no more urgent task before us than that of increasing output. But the little word "if" makes all the difference. If only socialism had come into being peacefully, in the way the capitalist gentlemen did not want to see it born. But there was a slight hitch. Even if there had been no war, the capitalist gentlemen would have done all in their power to prevent such a peaceful evolution. Great revolutions, even when they commence peacefully, as was the case with the great French Revolution, end in furious wars which are instigated by the counter-revolutionary bourgeoisie. Nor can it be otherwise, if we look at it from the point of view of the class struggle and not from the point of view of philistine phrase-mongering about liberty, equality, labour democracy and the will of the majority, of all the dull-witted, philistine phrase-mongering to which the Mensheviks, Socialist-Revolutionaries and all these "democrats" treat us. There can be no peaceful evolution towards socialism. In the present period, after the imperialist war, it is ridiculous to expect peaceful evolution, especially in a ruined country. Take France. France is one of the victors, and yet the production of grain there has dropped to half. In Britain they are saying that they are now paupers—I read this in an English bourgeois newspaper. And yet the Communists in a ruined country are blamed because industry is at a standstill! Whoever says this is either an utter idiot—even if he thrice calls himself a leader of the Berne International—or else a traitor to the workers.

The primary task in a ruined country is to save the working people. The primary productive force of human society as a whole, is the workers, the working people. If they survive, we shall save and restore everything.

We shall have to put up with many years of poverty, retrogression to barbarism. The imperialist war has thrown us back to barbarism; but if we save the working people, if we save the primary productive force of human society—the workers—we shall recover everything, but if we fail to save them, we shall perish, so that those who are now shouting about "consumers'", or "soldiers'", communism, who look down upon others with contempt and imagine that they are superior to these Bolshevik Communists, are, I repeat, absolutely ignorant of political economy, and pick out passages from books like a scholar whose head is a card index box filled with quotations from books, which he picks out as he needs them; but if a new situation arises which is not described in any book, he becomes confused and grabs the wrong quotation from the box.

At the present time, when the country is ruined, our main and fundamental task is to save the lives of the workers, to save the workers, for the workers are dying because the factories are at a standstill, and the factories are at a standstill because there is no fuel, and because our production is all artificial, industry is isolated from raw material sources. It is the same thing all over the world. Raw materials for the Russian cotton mills must be transported from Egypt, America, or the nearer Turkestan. Try to obtain these when the counter-revolutionary gangs and the British forces have captured Ashkhabad and Krasnovodsk. Try to obtain them from

Egypt or America when the railways lie in ruins, when they are at a standstill because there is no coal.

We must save the workers even if they are unable to work. If we keep them alive for the next few years, we shall save the country, save society and socialism. If we don't, we shall slip back into wage-slavery. This is how things stand with the socialism that springs not from the imagination of a peaceful simpleton who calls himself a Social-Democrat, but from actual reality, from the fierce, desperately fierce class struggle. This is a fact. We must sacrifice everything to save the lives of the workers. And in the light of this, when people come to us and say they are in favour of the equality of labour democracy, whereas the Communists do not even allow equality between the workers and peasants, our answer is: the workers and peasants are equal as working people, but the well-fed grain profiteer is not the equal of the hungry worker. This is the only reason why our Constitution says that the. workers and peasants are not equal.

Do you say that they ought to be equal? Let us weigh and count it up. Take sixty peasants and ten workers. The sixty peasants possess surplus stocks of grain. They are clothed in rags, but they have bread. Take the ten workers. After the imperialist war they, too, are in rags, but they are also exhausted, they have no bread, fuel or raw materials. The factories are idle. Well, are they equal? Should the sixty peasants have the right to decide and the ten workers be obliged to obey? The great principle of equality, unity of labour democracy and deciding by a majority vote!

That is what they tell us. And we tell them that they are mere clowns who confuse the hunger problem and obscure it with their high-sounding phrases.

We ask you whether the workers in a ruined country where the factories are idle ought to submit to the decision of the majority of peasants when the latter refuse to deliver their surplus stocks of grain. Have they the right to take these surplus stocks, by force, if necessary, if there is no other way? Give us a straightforward answer! But when we get right down to brass tacks they begin to twist and wriggle.

Industry is ruined in all countries, and it will remain in that state for several years, because it is easy to set fire to factories or to flood mines, it is easy to blow up railway wagons and to wreck locomotives — any fool can do that, even if he calls himself a German or French officer, and is very efficient, especially when he has good instruments for causing explosions, good fire-arms, and so forth. But it is a very difficult matter to restore it all. That will take years.

The peasantry constitutes a special class. As working people, they are hostile to capitalist exploitation; but at the same time they are property-owners. For centuries the peasant has been brought up to believe that the grain is his and he is at liberty to sell it. "This is my right," each one thinks, "because it is the fruit of my labour, my sweat and blood." This mentality cannot be changed overnight. It can be changed only as a result of a long and stern struggle. Whoever imagines that socialism can be achieved by one person convincing another, and that one a third, is at best an infant, or else a political hypocrite; and, of course, the majority of those who speak on political platforms belong to the latter category.

The whole point is that the peasants are accustomed to having the right to trade in grain. After we had abolished the capitalist institutions we found that there was still another force which kept capitalism going — the force of habit. And the more resolutely we abolished the institutions on which capitalism was based, the more strongly we felt the effects of this other force on which capitalism was based — the force of habit. Under favourable circumstances, institutions can be smashed at one stroke; but habit, never, no matter how favourable circumstances may be. Although we have given all the land to the peasants, have liberated them from landed proprietorship, and have swept away everything that held them in bondage, they nevertheless continue to think that "freedom" means freedom to trade in grain; and they regard as tyranny the compulsory surrendering of surplus stocks of grain at fixed prices. Why, what do you mean by "surrender"? they ask indignantly, especially since our grain supply apparatus is still defective because the entire bourgeois intelligentsia is on the side of Sukharevka.[5] Naturally, this machinery has to rely on people who are only just learning, at best—if they are conscientious and devoted to their task—will learn their business in a few years, and until that time the machinery will be defective, and sometimes all sorts of rascals who call themselves Communists will find their way into it. This danger threatens every ruling party, the victorious proletariat of every country, for it is impossible either to break the resistance of the bourgeoisie or to build up efficient machinery overnight. We know perfectly well that the machinery of the Commissariat of Food is still bad. Recently a scientific statistical investigation was made into the food conditions of the workers in the non-agricultural gubernias. The investigation showed that the workers obtain half their food from the Commissariat of Food and the other half from the profiteers; for the first half they pay one-tenth of their total expenditure on food, and for the other half they pay nine-tenths.

The first half of the food supplies, collected and delivered by the Commissariat of Food, is badly collected, of course, but it is collected on socialist and not on capitalist lines. It is collected by defeating the profiteers, and not by compromising with them; it is collected by sacrificing all other interests in the world, including the interests of the formal "equality" which the Mensheviks, Socialist-Revolutionaries and Co. make so much fuss about, to the interests of the starving workers. You keep your "equality", gentlemen, and we shall keep our hungry workers we have saved from starvation. No matter how much the Mensheviks may accuse us of violating "equality", the fact is that we have solved half our food problem in spite of unprecedented and incredible difficulties. And we say that if sixty peasants have surplus stocks of grain and ten workers are starving, we must not talk about "equality" in general, or about "the equality of working people", but say that it is the bounden duty of the sixty peasants to submit to the decisions of the ten workers and to give them, or at least to loan them, their surplus stocks of grain.

The science of political economy, if anybody has learned anything from it, the history of revolution, the history of political evolution throughout the whole of the nineteenth century show that the peasants follow the lead of either the workers or the bourgeoisie. Nor can they do otherwise. Some democrats may, of course, take exception to this, others may think that, being a malicious Marxist, I am slandering the peasants. They say the peasants constitute the majority, they are working people, and yet cannot follow their own road. Why?

If you don't know why, I would say to such citizens, read the elements of Marx's political economy in Kautsky's popular exposition, think about the evolution of any of the great revolutions of the eighteenth and nineteenth centuries, about the political history of any country in the nineteenth century, and you will learn why. The economics of capitalist society are such that the ruling power can be only capital or the proletariat which has overthrown capital.

There are no other forces in the economics of this society.

A peasant is half worker and half huckster. He is a worker because he earns his bread by the sweat of his brow and is exploited by the landowners, capitalists and merchants. He is a huckster because he sells grain, an article of necessity, an article for which a man will give up all his possessions if there is a shortage of it. Hunger is no man's friend. People will pay a thousand rubles, any sum of money, will give up all their property, for bread.

The peasant cannot be blamed for this; he is living under a commodity economy and has been for scores and hundreds of years, and is accustomed to exchange grain for money. You cannot change a habit or abolish money overnight. To abolish money you must organise the distribution of products for hundreds of millions of people, and this is something that must take many years. And so, as long as the commodity system exists, as long as there are starving workers side by side with well-fed peasants who are concealing their surplus stocks of grain, the antagonism of workers' and peasants' interests will persist. And whoever attempts to use phrases like "freedom", "equality" and "labour democracy" to brush aside this real antagonism created by the actual state of affairs, is at best a mere phrase-monger, and at worst a hypocritical champion of capitalism. If capitalism defeats the revolution it will do so by taking advantage of the ignorance of the peasants, by bribing them and luring them with the prospect of a return to freedom of trade. Actually, the Mensheviks and Socialist-Revolutionaries side with capitalism against socialism.

The economic programme of Kolchak, Denikin and all the Russian white guards is freedom to trade. They understand this, and it is not their fault that Citizen Sher does not. The economic facts of life do not change because a certain party does not understand them. The slogan of the bourgeoisie is freedom to trade. Efforts are made to beguile the peasants by asking them whether it would not be better to live in the good old way? Whether it would not be better to live freely by the free sale of the fruits of farm labour? What could be fairer? This is what those who consciously support Kolchak say, and they are right from the point of view of the interests of capital. To restore the power of capital in Russia it is necessary to rely on tradition—on the prejudices of the peasants as against their common sense, on their old habits of trading on the open market, and it is necessary forcibly to crush the resistance of the workers. There is no other way. The Kolchaks are right from the point of view of capital; their economic and political programme ties up neatly, there are no loose ends; they know there is a connection between freedom for peasants to trade and shooting down the workers. They are connected even though Citizen Sher is unaware of it. Freedom to trade in grain is the economic programme of Kolchak; the shooting of tens of thousands of workers—as occurred in Finland—is a necessary means of realising this programme, because the workers will not voluntarily surrender their gains. The connection cannot be broken, yet the Mensheviks and Social-Revolutionaries, who are totally ignorant of economic science and politics, who, being terrified philistines, have forgotten the ABC of socialism, are trying to make us forget this connection by talking about "equality" and "freedom", by shouting about our violating the principle of equality of "labour democracy" and saying that our Constitution is "unfair".

The vote of one worker is equal to several peasant votes. Is that unfair?

No, in the period when it is necessary to overthrow capital it is quite fair. I know where you have borrowed your conception of fairness from; you have borrowed it from yesterday's capitalist era. The equality, the freedom of commodity owners—that is your conception of fairness. A petty-bourgeois survival of petty-bourgeois prejudices—that is what your fairness, your equality, your labour democracy amount to. We, however, subordinate fairness to the interests of defeating capital. And capital can be defeated only by the united efforts of the proletariat.

Can tens of millions of peasants be firmly united against capital, against freedom of trade, overnight? No, economic conditions would prevent it even if the peasants were quite free and much more cultured. It cannot be done because different economic conditions and long years of preparation are needed for this. And who will make these preparations? Either the proletariat or the bourgeoisie.

Owing to their economic status in bourgeois society the peasants must follow either the workers or the bourgeoisie. There is no middle way. They may waver, become confused, conjure up all sorts of things; they may blame, swear, curse the "bigoted" representatives of the proletariat and the "bigoted" representatives of the bourgeoisie and say that they are the minority. You may curse them, talk loud about the majority, about the broad universal character of your labour democracy, about pure democracy. There is no end to the number of words you can string together, but they will only serve to obscure the fact that if the peasants do not follow the lead of the workers they will follow the lead of the bourgeoisie. There is not, nor can there be, a middle course. And those people who in this most difficult period of transition in history, when the workers are hungry and their industry is at a standstill, do not help the workers to take grain at a fairer but not a "free" price, not at a capitalist, hucksters' price, are carrying out the Kolchak programme no matter how much they may deny this to themselves, and no matter how sincerely they may be convinced that they are carrying out their own programme conscientiously.

Achievements and Difficulties of the Soviet Government
Lenin Collected Work Volume 29, pages 55-88

It is now the right time, when we have succeeded in restoring the revolutionary International, the Communist International, when the Soviet form of the movement has itself become both the theoretical and practical programme of the entire Third International—now that this has been done it is appropriate to review the general course of development of the Soviets. What are the Soviets? What is the significance of this form, which was created by the masses, and was not invented by any individual?

It seems to me that the tasks now confronting us, the proletariat that has won power, can be appraised only from this angle, as can also the degree to which we have attempted to fulfil these tasks and the degree to which we have succeeded during the past year under the dictatorship of the proletariat in Russia.

Only in the light of the general role of the Soviets, of their general significance, of the place they occupy in world history, is it possible to understand the situation we found ourselves in, why we had to act in the way we did and in no other, and how, looking back, we must examine the correctness or incorrectness of the steps we took.

And we are now doubly in need of such a more general, broader, and more far-reaching outlook, because it is sometimes painful for Party people in Russia to see faults and defects and feel dissatisfied with their work, because the practical fulfilment of the urgent, current, immediate, everyday administrative duties that have been, and continue to be, the lot of the Soviet authorities often distracts attention, compels us, in spite of ourselves—it is no use rebelling against the conditions under which we have to work—to devote too much attention to the petty details of administration. They cause us to forget the general course of the world-wide development of the proletarian dictatorship, its evolution through Soviet power or, more correctly, the Soviet movement, through the groping of the proletarian masses within the Soviets—something we all experienced and have forgotten—and through the attempt to achieve the dictatorship within the Soviets.

These are the difficulties we have encountered and the general tasks to which, in my opinion, we must turn our attention so that we may as far as possible get away from the petty details of administration in which everybody who is engaged in practical local government work is absorbed, and so that we may understand what a long way we, as a contingent of the world proletarian army, have still to go.

Complete and final victory on a world scale cannot be achieved in Russia alone; it can be achieved only when the proletariat is victorious in at least all the advanced countries, or, at all events, in some of the largest of the advanced countries. Only then shall we be able to say with absolute confidence that the cause of the proletariat has triumphed, that our first objective—**the overthrow of capitalism—has been achieved.**

We have achieved this objective in one country, and this confronts us with a second task. Since Soviet power has been established, **since the bourgeoisie has been overthrown in one country**, the second task is to wage the struggle on a world scale, on a different plane, the struggle of the proletarian state surrounded by capitalist states.

This situation is an entirely novel and difficult one.

On the other hand, since the rule of the bourgeoisie has been overthrown, the main task is to organise the development of the country.

The yellow socialists who have gathered in Berne and now intend to honour us with a visit by distinguished foreigners, are extremely fond of repeating that "the Bolsheviks believe in the almighty power of violence". This phrase only shows that those who use it are people, who in the heat of the revolutionary struggle, when they are being completely crushed by the violence of the bourgeoisie—look at what is going on in Germany—are incapable of teaching their own proletariat the tactics of necessary violence.

Under certain circumstances violence is both necessary and useful, but there are circumstances under which violence cannot produce results. There have been cases, however, of not everyone appreciating this difference, so that it must be discussed. In October violence—the overthrow of the bourgeoisie by Soviet power, the removal of the old government, revolutionary violence—resulted in a brilliant success.

Why? First, because the masses were organised in Soviets, and secondly, because in the long political period, from February to October, the position of the enemy—the bourgeoisie—was undermined, sapped, washed away, like a block of ice by the spring thaw, and internally had been deprived of his strength; and the movement in October, compared, say, with the present revolutionary movement in Germany, brought us such a complete and brilliant victory for revolutionary violence.

May we assume that such a path, such a form of struggle, such an easy victory for revolutionary violence, is possible if these conditions do not exist?

It would be a very great mistake to assume that. And the greater the revolutionary victories achieved under certain specific conditions the more often does the danger arise of our allowing ourselves to be flattered by such victories and not stopping to think coolly, calmly and attentively, about the conditions that made them possible.

When we tore the Kerensky government and Milyukov's coalition ministry to shreds, so to speak, compelled them to shuffle portfolios over and over again, compelled them to play ministerial leapfrog from right to left, from left to right, up and down and down and up, it became obvious that they could not pull together, no matter in what order they sat, and then they were blown away like so much chaff.

Is the situation that now confronts our practical tasks in respect of world imperialism anything like that? Of course not.

That is why the Treaty of Brest created serious difficulties in the sphere of foreign policy, but the mass character of the movement helped us to overcome them.

But what is the source of the mistakes that caused some of our comrades to think that we were committing a heinous crime? There is still an odd crank or two among people able to wield the pen who imagine that they are somebodies, that they have experience, can teach others, and so forth, who even now assert that this was a compromise with German imperialism.

Yes, we made the same compromise when we "compromised" with the tsar by entering the disgusting, reactionary Duma and undermining it from within.

Can we count on the overthrow of world imperialism merely by force before the proletariat in those imperialist countries has reached the necessary stage of development?

If the question is presented in this way—and we as Marxists have always taught that this is the only way to present the question—we must agree that it would be very absurd and foolish to employ the policy of violence under those circumstances, and complete failure to understand the conditions under which a policy of violence can be successful.

Now we realise this; we have gained experience.

While we, at the time of the Treaty of Brest, were obliged to muster our forces and amidst the most extraordinary difficulties lay the foundations of a new army, the Red Army, in a country ruined and exhausted by war to a greater degree than any other country in the world, while we, in the first half and the beginning of the second half of 1918, were, stone by stone, laying the foundations of a genuine socialist Red Army, the imperialism of other countries was being sapped by internal disintegration and the growing discontent, and was becoming enfeebled.

And revolutionary violence triumphed in Germany after many months of development of the struggle had sapped the strength of imperialism in that country; and the same thing is now being repeated to some extent—to some extent, but not entirely—in the Entente countries.

An American who had watched events in the West-European countries very closely, at first hand, and without prejudice, said to me recently, "France is undoubtedly on the eve of a great disappointment, the collapse of illusions. The French people are being fed with promises—you are the victors, they are told." The bourgeoisie is taking advantage of the old patriotic sentiments of the entire French nation, of their anger at the way they were crushed in 1870, and of their fury at the way the country has been depopulated, bled white and exhausted by four years of war—the bourgeoisie is taking advantage of all this to divert these sentiments into chauvinist channels: "We have beaten the Germans; our pockets will now be filled, and we shall be able to relax." But the dispassionate American, looking at things like a businessman, says, "The Germans will not pay, for they have nothing to pay with."

That is why the French nation is being fed with promises and fairy-tales about the peace, the final victory, that is coming soon. But peace means the collapse of all hopes of being able to crawl out of this bloody mire at least partly alive—with broken arms and legs, but alive. It will be impossible to crawl out of this peace while the old capitalist system is intact, because the war has piled up such a heap of debts, such a mass of ruins throughout the capitalist world, that it is impossible to crawl out of it without upsetting the whole pile and starting an avalanche.

Even those who are not revolutionaries, who have no faith in revolution, and dread it, are nevertheless discussing it theoretically and will be convinced by the course of events, by the consequences of the imperialist war, that there is no way out except revolution.

I repeat, I was particularly astonished by the American's appraisal of the situation from the point of view of a business man who, of course, has not studied the theory of the class struggle and sincerely thinks it is nonsense, but who is interested in millions and thousands of millions, and being able to count, asks: "Will they pay or not?" And he answers, again from the shrewd businessman's point of view: "They have nothing to pay with! You will not even get 20 kopeks in the ruble!

It is in such a situation in all the Entente countries that we see profound and widespread unrest stimulated by the workers' sympathy for the Soviet form.

A Paris crowd, for example, is perhaps more sensitive than any assembly of people in any other country, because the people there have had a very good schooling, they have made a number of revolutions—and there, this most responsive crowd, which will not allow a speaker to strike a false note, now interrupts those who dare to say anything against the Bolsheviks. And yet, only a few months ago, nobody could even as much as hint that he is in favour of Bolshevism without being jeered at by the very same crowd.

Meanwhile the Paris bourgeoisie has set its entire machine of lies, slander and deception in motion against Bolshevism. But now we know what this means, for in 1917 we Bolsheviks experienced the persecution of the entire bourgeois press. The bourgeoisie in our country, however, miscalculated slightly and overdid it in thinking that they could enmesh the Bolsheviks in their net of slander; they overdid things so badly, they went so far in their attacks that they gave us a free advertisement and compelled even the most backward workers to say to themselves: "Well, if the capitalists are abusing the Bolsheviks so much, it shows that those Bolsheviks know how to fight the capitalists!"

That is why the policy which we were obliged to pursue at the time of the Brest peace, a most brutal, violent and humiliating peace, proved to be the only correct policy that could have been pursued.

And I think that it will be useful to recall this policy once again at the present time when a similar situation is arising in the Entente countries, when there, too, the bourgeoisie is filled with a mad desire to thrust their debts, poverty and ruin on Russia, to plunder Russia and crush her in order to divert the rising anger of the masses of their own working people from themselves.

Looking at the situation dispassionately we must say to ourselves very clearly, if we do not want to fool ourselves and others—this is a dangerous thing for revolutionaries to indulge in—we must say that as far as military strength is concerned, the Entente is stronger than we are. But if we look at things in the light of their development, we shall also say very definitely and with a conviction based not only on our revolutionary views but also on our experience, that the strength of the Entente countries will not last, they are on the threshold of a great and abrupt change in the temper of their masses.

They have been feeding both French and British workers with promises, saying, "We shall finish plundering the whole world and you will have enough to eat." This is what the bourgeois press is shouting and dinning into the ears of the ignorant masses.

They will probably conclude peace in a few months—if they do not quarrel among themselves in the meantime, and there are a number of serious symptoms that this is possible. But if they succeed in concluding peace without flying at each other's throats, this peace will be the beginning of an immediate collapse, because these unprecedented debts cannot be paid, and they can do nothing to alleviate the desperate state of ruin, when in France the production of wheat has dropped to less than half and famine is knocking at the door everywhere, and the productive forces have been destroyed; they are unable to do anything about it.

If we look at the situation soberly we shall have to admit that the method of appraising affairs which proved so correct in appraising the Russian revolution is, day after day, indicating the coming of the world revolution. We know that the streams that will carry with them the icebergs of the Entente, of capitalism, of imperialism, are gaining strength day after day.

On the one hand, the Entente countries are stronger than we are; but on the other hand, they-cannot possibly hold out long owing to the internal situation.

It is this situation that determines the intricate tasks of international policy—tasks which we may, and probably will, have to tackle in the very near future, and which, though I am insufficiently informed about them in all their detail, I would like to talk to you-about most of all so that a picture of the experience of the work done by the Council of People's Commissars, work in the sphere of foreign policy, will be presented to you, comrades, in a clear and interesting form.

The most important of our experiences is the Brest peace. This is the most significant result of the foreign policy of the Council of People's Commissars. We were obliged to play for time, to retreat, manoeuvre and sign a most humiliating peace treaty, and in this way gain an opportunity to lay the foundation of a new socialist army. This foundation we have laid, while our once mighty and all-powerful enemy is already powerless.

All over the world things are moving in the same direction, and this is the chief and principal lesson that we must learn and try to understand as clearly as possible in order to avoid making mistakes in the extremely intricate, extremely difficult and extremely involved problems of foreign policy which any day may confront the Council of People's Commissars, the Central Executive Committee, and Soviet power as a whole.

I shall conclude my remarks on foreign policy with this and proceed to deal with some other extremely important questions.

Comrades, as regards activities in the military field—a year ago, in February and March 1918, we had no army at all. We had, perhaps, ten million armed workers and peasants who constituted the old army that had collapsed completely, was fully ready and determined to desert, to flee, to abandon everything, come what may.

At that time this was regarded as an exclusively Russian phenomenon. People thought that owing to the Russians' characteristic impatience, or lack of organisation, they would not hold out, whereas the Germans would.

That is what we were told. And now we see that a few months have passed and the same thing has happened to the German army, which was immeasurably superior to ours in culture, equipment, and discipline, in providing decent conditions for the sick and wounded, as regards home leave, and so forth. Even the most cultured and disciplined masses could not stand the slaughter, the many years of slaughter, and so a period of absolute disintegration set in when even the advanced German army broke down.

Evidently, there is a limit not only for Russia but for all countries. There are different limits for different countries, but for all of them there is a limit beyond which it is impossible to continue to wage war for the sake of the interests of the capitalists. This is what we see today.

German imperialism has completely exposed itself as a predator. The most important thing is that even in America and in France, in these notorious democracies (the traitors to socialism, the Mensheviks and Socialist-Revolutionaries, those hapless people who call themselves socialists, are fond of chattering about democracies), in these most advanced democracies of the world, in these republics, imperialism is becoming more arrogant every day and we find there beasts of prey more predatory than anywhere else. They are plundering the world, fighting each other, and arming against each other. This cannot be concealed for long. It could be concealed when the war fever was at its height. But the fever is subsiding, peace is approaching, and it is precisely in these democracies that the masses see, in spite of all the lies they are being told, that the war has led to fresh plunder, that the most democratic republic is nothing more nor less than a disguise for the most brutal and cynical predator who is ready to ruin hundreds of millions of people in order to pay the debts, that is, to pay the imperialist gentlemen, the capitalists, for being good enough to allow the workers to cut each other's throats. This is becoming clearer to the masses every day.

It is this situation that makes possible political statements such as the article written by the military correspondent of a newspaper that belongs to the richest and most politically experienced bourgeoisie, the London Times ; the author appraises events by saying that all over the world the armies are breaking up and there is only one country where the army is being built up, and that country is Russia.

The bourgeoisie—which militarily is far stronger than Soviet Bolshevism—is compelled to admit this fact. And this fact serves as a criterion of what we have accomplished in the course of our Soviet activities in the past year.

We succeeded in reaching a turning-point where instead of an army of ten million, the bulk of which had deserted, unable to stand the horrors of war, and which had realised that this was a criminal war, we began to build, one hundred thousand after another, a socialist army, which knows what it is fighting for and is ready to make greater sacrifices and suffer more privation than under tsarism. For this army knows that it is fighting for its own cause, for its own land, for its own power in the factories, that it is defending the power of the working people, and that the working people of other countries are awakening, slowly and with great difficulty, but awakening, nevertheless.

This is the situation that characterises the years' experience of Soviet power.

War is an incredible hardship for Soviet Russia, war is an incredible hardship for a people who for four years have borne the horrors of the imperialist war. For Soviet Russia war is an incredibly heavy burden. But at the present time even our powerful enemies admit that their armies are cracking up, whereas our army is being built. For the first time in history an army is being built on the basis of the closest contact, inseverable contact, coalescence, one might say, of the army and the Soviets. The Soviets unite all the working people, all the exploited, and the army is being built up for the purpose of socialist defence and on the basis of class-consciousness.

An eighteenth-century Prussian monarch once wisely remarked: "If our soldiers knew what we were fighting for, it would be impossible to wage a single war." That old Prussian monarch was no fool. We, however, are prepared to say, comparing our position with that of the monarch, that we can wage war because the masses know what they are fighting for; and they want to fight notwithstanding the incredible burdens—burdens, I repeat, far greater than under tsarism—knowing that they are making these desperate and incredibly heavy sacrifices in defence of their socialist cause, fighting side by side with those workers of other countries who are "disintegrating" and are beginning to understand our position.

Some foolish people are shouting about red militarism. These are political crooks who pretend that they believe this absurdity and throw charges of this kind right and left, exercising their lawyers' skill in concocting plausible arguments and in throwing dust in the eyes of the masses. And the Mensheviks and Socialist-

Revolutionaries shout: "Look, instead of socialism, they are giving you red militarism!"

What a "horrible" crime, indeed! The imperialists of the whole world hurled themselves upon the Russian Republic in order to crush it, and we began to form an army which for the first time in history knows what it is fighting for and what it is making sacrifices for, which is successfully contending against a numerically superior enemy, and which with every month of its resistance on an unprecedented scale is bringing nearer the world revolution, and this is denounced as red militarism!

I repeat, these are either fools to whom no political appraisal can apply, or else political crooks.

Everybody knows that this war was forced upon us. We brought the old war to a close at the beginning of 1918, and did not start a new war. Everybody knows that the white guards attacked us in the West, South and East, only because they were assisted by the Entente, which scattered millions right and left. And these advanced countries collected and handed over to the whiteguards the vast stocks of war supplies and ammunition left over from the imperialist war, for those gentlemen, the millionaires and multimillionaires, know that their fate is being decided here, that it is here they will perish if they do not crush us at once.

The socialist, republic is straining every nerve, is making sacrifices and winning victories. And if after a year of civil war you look at the map and compare what Soviet Russia was in March 1918 and in July 1918—when the German imperialists in the West occupied the line laid down by the Treaty of Brest, when the Ukraine was under the heel of the German imperialists, when the Czechoslovaks, bribed by the French and British, lorded it in the East as far as Kazan and Simbirsk—if you look at the map today, you will see that we have expanded immensely, that we have won enormous victories.

Is this situation, only sordid and despicable political crooks can use strong language and accuse us of red militarism.

Never in history has there been a revolution in which it was possible to lay down one's arms and rest on one's laurels after the victory. Whoever thinks that such revolutions are possible is not only no revolutionary, but the worst enemy of the working class. There has never been a revolution, even a second-rate one, even a bourgeois revolution in which the only issue was the transfer of power from one propertied minority to another. We know of examples! The French revolution, against which the old powers hurled themselves at the beginning of the nineteenth century in order to crush it, we call great precisely because it succeeded in rousing the vast masses of the people in defence of its gains and they resisted the whole world; this was one of its greatest merits.

Revolutions are subjected to the most serious tests in the fire of battle. If you are oppressed and exploited and think of throwing off the power of the exploiters, if you are deter- mined to carry this to its logical conclusion, you must understand that you will have to contend against the onslaught of the exploiters of the whole world. If you are ready to offer resistance and to make further sacrifices in order to hold out in the struggle, you are a revolutionary; if not, you will be crushed.

This is how the question is presented by the history of all revolutions.

The real test to which our revolution is being subjected is that we, in a backward country, succeeded in capturing power before the others, succeeded in establishing the Soviet form of government, the power of the working and exploited people. Shall we be able to hold, on at least until the masses in the other countries make a move? If we are not prepared to make fresh sacrifices and do not hold out, it will be said that our revolution was historically unjustified. But democrats in civilised countries who are armed to the teeth dread the presence of a hundred or so Bolsheviks in a free republic with a hundred million population, in the way America does. Bolshevism is so infectious! And it turns out that the democrats cannot cope with a hundred immigrants from starving, ruined Russia who might talk about Bolshevism! The masses sympathise with us! The bourgeoisie have only one path of salvation, and that is, while their hand still grasps the sword, while they still control the guns, to turn these guns against Soviet Russia and to crush her in a few months, because later on nothing will crush her. This is the situation we are in; this is what determined the military policy of the Council of People's Commissars during the past year; and this is why, pointing to the facts, to the results, we have a right to say that we have stood the test only because the workers and peasants, though utterly exhausted by war, are creating a new army under still more arduous conditions and are displaying new heroism.

That is a brief summary of the policy of the Soviet government in the military field. Permit me to say just a few more words about a matter in which military policy overlaps policy in another field — economic policy. I refer to the military experts.

You are probably aware of the controversy that has arisen over this question, and that some comrades, most devoted and convinced Bolshevik Communists, often expressed vehement protests against the fact that for the purpose of organising our socialist Red Army we are utilising the services of the old military experts, tsarist generals and officers, whose records are blemished by their service to the tsar, and in some cases by the bloody acts of repression against workers and peasants.

The contradiction here is glaring, and indignation, one might say, springs up of its own accord. How can we build a socialist army with the aid of tsarist experts?!

It turned out that this was the way, the only way, we did build up an army. If we give some thought to the task that has fallen to our lot, it will not be difficult to understand that it is the only way we could build it. This is not only a military matter, it is a task that confronts us in all spheres of everyday life, and of the country's economy.

The old utopian socialists imagined that socialism could be built by men of a new type, that first they would train good, pure and splendidly educated people, and these would build socialism. We always laughed at this and said that this was playing with puppets, that it was socialism as an amusement for young ladies, but not serious politics.

We want to build socialism with the aid of those men and women who grew up under capitalism, were depraved and corrupted by capitalism, but steeled for the struggle by capitalism. There are proletarians who have been so hardened that they can stand a thousand times more hardship than any army. There are tens of millions of oppressed peasants, ignorant and scattered, but capable of uniting around the proletariat in the struggle, if the proletariat adopts skillful tactics. And there are scientific and technical experts all thoroughly imbued with the bourgeois world outlook, there are military experts who were trained under bourgeois conditions—if they were only bourgeois it would not be so bad, but there were also conditions of landed proprietorship, serfdom and the big stick. As far as concerns the economy, all the agronomists, engineers and school-teachers were recruited from the propertied class; they did not drop from the skies. Neither under the reign of Tsar Nicholas nor under the Republican President Wilson were the propertyless proletarians at the bench and the peasants at the plough able to get a university education. Science and technology exist only for the rich, for the propertied class; capitalism provides culture only for the minority. We must build socialism out of this culture; we have no other material. We want to start building socialism at once out of the material that capitalism left us yesterday to be used today, at this very moment, and not with people reared in hothouses, assuming that we were to take this fairy-tale seriously. We have bourgeois experts and nothing else. We have no other bricks with which to build. Socialism must triumph, and we socialists and

Communists must prove by deeds that we are capable of building socialism with these bricks, with this material, that we are capable of building socialist society with the aid of proletarians who have enjoyed the fruits of culture only to an insignificant degree, and with the aid of bourgeois specialists.

If you do not build communist society with this material, you will prove that you are mere phrase-mongers and windbags.

This is how the question is presented by the historical legacy of world capitalism! This is the difficulty that confronted us concretely when we took power, when we set up the Soviet machinery of state!

This is only half the task, but it is the greater half. Soviet machinery of state means that the working people are united in such a way as to crush capitalism by the weight of their mass unity. The masses did this. But it is not enough to crush capitalism. We must take the entire culture that capitalism left behind and build socialism with it. We must take all its science, technology, knowledge and art. Without these we shall be unable to build communist society. But this science, technology and art are in the hands and in the heads of the experts.

This is the task that confronts us in all spheres. It is a task with inherent contradictions, like the inherent contradictions of capitalism as a whole. It is a most difficult task, but a practicable one. We cannot wait twenty years until we have trained pure, communist experts, until we have trained the first generation of Communists without blemish and without reproach. No, excuse me, but we must build now, in two months and not in twenty years' time, so as to be able to fight the bourgeoisie, to oppose the bourgeois science and technology of the whole world. Here we must achieve victory. It is difficult to make the bourgeois experts serve us by the weight of our masses, but it is possible, and if we do it, we shall triumph.

When Comrade Trotsky informed me recently that the number of officers of the old army employed by our War Department runs into several tens of thousands, I perceived concretely where the secret of using our enemy lay, how to compel those who had opposed communism to build it, how to build communism with the bricks which the capitalists had chosen to hurl against us! We have no other bricks! And so, we must compel the bourgeois experts, under the leadership of the proletariat, to build up our edifice with these bricks. This is what is difficult; but this is the pledge of victory.

Naturally, on this path, which is a new and difficult one, we have made more than a few mistakes; on this path we have met with more than a few reverses. Everybody knows that a certain number of experts have systematically betrayed us. Among the experts in the factories, among the agronomists, and in the administration, we have seen and see today at every step a malicious attitude to work, malicious sabotage.

We know that all this presents tremendous difficulties and that we cannot achieve victory by violence alone. . . . We, of course, are not opposed to violence. We laugh at those who are opposed to the dictatorship of the proletariat, we laugh and say that they are fools who do not understand that there must be either the dictatorship of the proletariat or the dictatorship of the bourgeoisie. Those who think otherwise are either idiots or are so politically ignorant that it would be a disgrace to allow them to come anywhere near a meeting, let alone on the platform. The only alternative is either violence against Liebknecht and Luxemburg, the murder of the best leaders of the workers, or the violent suppression of the exploiters; and whoever dreams of a middle course is our most harmful and dangerous enemy. That is how the matter stands at present. Hence, when we talk of utilising the services of the experts we must bear in mind the lesson taught by Soviet policy during the past year. During that year we have broken and defeated the exploiters and we must now solve the prob- lem of using the bourgeois specialists. Here, I repeat, violence alone will get us nowhere. Here, in addition to violence, after successful violence, we need the organisation, discipline and moral weight of the victorious proletariat, which will subordinate all the bourgeois experts to its will and draw them into its work.

Some people may say that Lenin is recommending moral persuasion instead of violence! But it is foolish to imagine that we can solve the problem of organising a new science and technology for the development of communist society by violence alone. That is nonsense! We, as a Party, as people who have learned something during this year of Soviet activity, will not be so foolish as to think so, and we will warn the masses not to think so. The employment of all the institutions of bourgeois capitalist society requires not only the successful use of violence, but also organisation, discipline, comradely discipline among the masses, the organisation of proletarian influence over the rest of the population, the creation of a new, mass environment, which will convince the bourgeois specialists that they have no alternative, that there can be no return to the old society, and that they can do their work only in conjunction with the Communists who are working by their side, who are leading the masses, who enjoy the absolute confidence of the masses, and whose object is to ensure that the fruits of bourgeois science and technology, the fruits of thousands of years of the development of civilisation, shall be enjoyed not by a handful of people for the purpose of distinguishing themselves and amassing wealth, but by literally all the working people.

This is an immensely difficult task, the fulfilment of which will require decades! But to carry it out ,we must create a force, a discipline, comradely discipline, Soviet discipline, proletarian discipline, such as will not only physically crush the counter-revolutionary bourgeoisie, but also encompass them completely, subordinate them to our will, compel them to proceed along our lines, to serve our cause.

I repeat that we come up against this problem every day is the work of organising our military forces, in the work of economic development, in the work of every economic council, in the work of every factory committee and of every nationalised factory. There was hardly a week during all past year that the Council of People's Commissars did not discuss and settle this question in one way or another. I am sure that there was not a single factory committee in Russia, not a single agricultural commune, not a single state farm, not a single uyezd land department which did not come up against this issue scores of times in the course of the past year's Soviet activity.

This is what makes this task so difficult, but it is also what makes it a really gratifying one. This is what we must do now, the day after the exploiters were crushed by the force of the proletarian insurrection. We suppressed their resistance—this had to be done. But this is not the only thing that has to be done. By the force of the new organisation, the comradely organisation of the working people, we must compel them to serve us. We must cure them of their old vices and prevent them from relapsing into their exploiting practices. They have remained bourgeois, and they occupy posts as commanders and staff officers in our army, as engineers and agronomists, and these old, bourgeois people call themselves Mensheviks and Socialist-Revolutionaries. It does not matter what they call themselves. They are bourgeois through and through, from head to foot, in their outlook and in their habits.

Well, what shall we do, throw them out? You cannot throw out hundreds of thousands! And if we did we should be harming only ourselves. We have no other material with which to build communism than that created by capitalism. We must not throw them out, but break their resistance, watch them at every step, make no political concessions to them, which spineless people are inclined to do every minute. Educated people yield to the policy and influence of the bourgeoisie because they acquired all their education in a bourgeois environment and from that environment.

That is why they stumble at every step and make political concessions to the counter-revolutionary bourgeoisie.

A Communist who says that he must not get into a state where he will soil his hands, that he must have clean, communist hands, and that he will build communist society with clean communist hands and scorn the services of the contemptible, counter-revolutionary bourgeois co-operators, is a mere phrase-monger, because we cannot help resorting to their services.

The practical task that confronts us now is to enlist the services of all those whom capitalism has trained to oppose us, to watch them day after day, to place worker commissars over them in an environment of communist organisation, day after day to thwart their counter-revolutionary designs, and at the same time to learn from them.

The science which we, at best, possess, is the science of the agitator and propagandist, of the man who has been steeled by the hellishly hard lot of the factory worker, or starving peasant, a science which teaches us how to hold out for a long time and to persevere in the struggle, and this has saved us up to now. All this is necessary, but it is not enough. With this alone we cannot triumph. In order that our victory may be complete and final we must take all that is valuable from capitalism, take all its science and culture.

How can we take it? We must learn from them, from our enemies. Our advanced peasants, the class-conscious workers in their factories, our officials in the uyezd land departments must learn from the bourgeois agronomists, engineers, and others, so as to acquire the fruits of their culture.

In this respect, the struggle that flared up in our Party during the past year was extremely useful. It gave rise to numerous sharp collisions, but there are no struggles without sharp collisions. As a result, however, we gained practical experience in a matter that had never before confronted us but without which it is impossible to achieve communism. I say again that the task of combining the victorious proletarian revolution with bourgeois culture, with bourgeois science and technology, which up to now has been available to few people, is a difficult one. Here, everything depends on the organisation and discipline of the advanced sections of the working people. If, in Russia, the millions of downtrodden and ignorant peasants who are totally incapable of independent development, who were oppressed by the landowners for centuries, did not have at their head, and by their side an advanced section of the urban workers whom they understood, with whom they were intimate, who enjoyed their confidence, whom they believed as fellow-workers, if there were not this organisation which is capable of rallying the masses of the working people, of influencing them, of explaining to them and convincing them of the importance of the task of taking over the entire bourgeois culture, the cause of communism would be hopeless.

I say this not from the abstract point of view, but from the point of view of a whole year's daily experience. Although this experience includes a multitude of petty details, sometimes dull and unpleasant, we must learn to see something deeper in them. We must understand that these petty details, these conflicts between, say, a factory committee and an engineer, a Red Army man and some bourgeois officer, a peasant and a bourgeois agronomist— these conflicts, this friction, these petty details contain much that is immeasurably deeper. We have vanquished the prejudice that these bourgeois specialists should be thrown out. We have taken over this machine, it is still running badly, we have no illusions on that score; it keeps stopping, it makes mistakes all the time, it runs into ditches, and we drag it out again, but it is moving, and we shall keep it on the right road. This is the only way we can emerge from this quagmire of destruction, frightful difficulties, ruin, barbarism, poverty and starvation into which we were dragged by the war, and into which the imperialists of all countries are trying to push us and keep us.

But we have begun to emerge, the first steps have been taken.

This year of Soviet activity has taught us clearly to understand the task in every individual case of work in the factories and among the peasants, and we have mastered it. Soviet power has gained tremendously by it in the past year, and it has been worth while spending a year on it. We shall not, as we did in the old days, discuss theoretically and in general terms the importance of bourgeois specialists and the importance of proletarian organisations, but at every step, in every factory committee, and in every land organisation, we shall make use of the experience we have gained. We have laid the foundation of our Red Army, we now have a small foundation, we now have nationalised factories where the workers understand their tasks and have begun to increase labour productivity with the aid of bourgeois specialists (who at every step are trying to turn to the past while the mass organisations of the workers are compelling them to march forward in step with Soviet power)—all this is a great gain for Soviet power. This work is imperceptible, there is nothing brilliant about it, it is difficult to appraise its real value, but the very fact that from simply suppressing the exploiters we have advanced to a phase where we are learning ourselves and teaching the masses how to build communism with capitalist bricks and compel the capitalist bourgeois specialists to work for us, is a step forward for our movement. Only on this road shall we achieve victory. And now we know that if we proceed as we have been up to now we shall really achieve this victory.

Comrades, I now come to the last question that I want to deal with, if only briefly, for I have already spoken too long. I have in mind the question of our relations with the countryside.

Up to now I have spoken about our activities in the military field, about the dictatorship, and about utilising the services of bourgeois specialists. Now I want to deal with another great difficulty that we encounter in our work of communist construction.

What is to be done if the proletariat has taken power in a country where the urban proletariat constitutes a minority of the

128

population, while the majority are peasants accustomed to work individually and deeply imbued with habits of individual farming?

The majority of these peasants, however, have been so ruined, impoverished and exhausted by the oppression of the landowners and capitalists that they willingly render assistance to the proletariat. When an urban worker approaches a peasant in a reasonable way, tactfully, as man to man, and not as if he wants to be a boss, which arouses legitimate hatred, he wins the peasant's most comradely confidence and complete support. We know that this is a fact, and Soviet power in the villages is based on it. Soviet power has been able to hold out only because it has been receiving the sincere support of the majority of the working people. We have been receiving this support because the urban workers have established contact with the rural poor in thousands of ways, of which we have not even an inkling.

The state, which formerly hindered the establishment of such contacts, is now doing all it can to facilitate it. This alone explains why Soviet power has been able to hold out and this is the sole pledge of victory.

The enormous difficulties I have just referred to are due to the peasants being accustomed to work individually and to sell their grain freely. They think this is quite legitimate. They argue as follows. How can it be that having worked so hard to produce grain at the cost of so much sweat and blood, we have no right to sell it as we please? The peasants consider themselves the injured party.

But we know from the entire development of Russia that freedom to trade means freely breeding capitalists; and freedom to trade in a country which has been exhausted by starvation, where starving people are prepared to give anything, even to sell themselves into slavery, for a crust of bread, freedom to trade when the country is starving means allowing the minority freely to amass wealth and ruin the majority.

We must prove that help for the peasantry is a primary task in a country which has been exhausted by starvation; but we can help the peasantry only by uniting their activities, by uniting the masses, for the peasants are scattered, disunited and accustomed to work and live out of contact with one another.

There are no objective obstacles to the fulfilment of this difficult task. All that had to be done by means of force, has been done; we do not reject force, for we know that there are kulaks among the peasants who are actively resisting us and go to the length of organising white guard revolts. This, however, does not apply to peasants in the mass. The kulaks are a minority. As far as they are concerned, the only thing to do is to fight them and to keep on fighting them. They must be crushed, and we are crushing them. But after the successful fulfilment of the task of crushing the rural exploiters problems arise which cannot be solved by the use of force. In this sphere, as in all the others, we can fulfil our task only by means of mass organisation, by means of the prolonged educational influence of the urban proletariat over the peasantry.

Shall we succeed in this tasks? Yes, we know from experience that we shall, and only because the vast majority of the peasants have confidence in the workers' government and on the basis of this confidence in the workers we can reinforce the foundation we have begun to build, and which we must continue to build, but only by means of comradely influence and discipline.

This is the practical task that now confronts us.

When we established the Poor Peasants Committees,[1] when we tried to introduce barter with the rural districts, we did so not to enable the rich peasants to obtain goods, but primarily to enable the poor peasants to obtain the small quantities of goods that the cities could provide so that by helping the poor we would be able with their aid to beat the kulaks and take their surplus grain.

It has been an extremely difficult task to supply grain to the population of a vast country with poor transport facilities and a scattered peasantry, and it has given us the most trouble. I recall all the meetings of the Council of People's Commissars and must say that the Soviet government has not worked so persistently on anything as it has on this. Our peasants are extremely scattered and disunited. In the rural districts ignorance and the habit of working individually are more deep rooted than anywhere: The rural population is dissatisfied with not being allowed freedom to trade in grain. And in this situation, of course, political crooks, all sorts of Socialist-Revolutionaries and Mensheviks, incite the peasantry by saying to them, "They are robbing you!"

There are scoundrels who after a year of Soviet activity when, incidentally, food supply authorities have shown that during the past few months we supplied the rural districts with 42,000 carloads of goods and received in exchange only 39,000 carloads of grain—there are scoundrels, I say, who, after this come along and yell, "Peasants, the Soviet government is robbing you!"

At a time when the workers in the towns are on the verge of exhaustion—and nowhere is there such terrible hunger as in the towns and in the non-agricultural parts of Russia—when the peasants have taken all the land and grain that belonged to landowners, and when the bulk of the peasants, as we know, in the first year of Soviet power worked for themselves and not for the landowners and merchants and are now feeding better than they did before, when the population of the urban and non-agricultural districts of the country is starving and all the capitalists are trying to crush us by famine, at such a time people wearing Menshevik, Socialist- Revolutionary, or other clownish costumes, have the insolence to shout, "They are robbing you!" These people are agents of capitalism, and we must treat them as such and nothing else!

At a time when the main difficulty confronting the Soviet government is the famine, it is the duty of every Soviet citizen to hand over all his surplus grain to the famine-stricken. This is so clear and obvious, so intelligible to every working man, that nobody can say a word against it. One must be a scoundrel, a political crook, to obscure this plain, clear and obvious truth, to make it unintelligible, or distort it!

It is on this truth that the urban workers rely. It is because this truth is so obvious that they are able to do their extremely difficult job. Up to now they have told the poor peasants that they and the workers constitute the real bulwark of Soviet power, that is why the working class has established Poor Peasants' Committees, organised barter, and made it obligatory for the co-operatives to include the whole population. All the decrees on agriculture issued up to now have this main idea running through them. And in all our appeals to the urban workers we have said, "Unite with the rural poor, for unless you do, you will be unable to solve the most important and most difficult problem, namely, the bread problem." And to the peasants we said, "Either you unite with the urban workers, in which case we shall triumph; or you allow yourselves to be misled by the admonitions and exhortations of the capitalists and their servants and flunkeys in Menshevik garb, who say, "Don't let the towns rob you, trade as you please, the rich get richer, what do you care if people are dying of starvation', in which case you yourselves will perish, you will become the slaves of the capitalists and cause the ruin of Soviet Russia." It was only under capitalism that people argued, "I shall trade, I shall get rich. Every man for himself and God for all." This was the principle of capitalism and it engendered war; that is why the workers and peasants were poor, and an insignificant number of people became multimillionaires.

The problem is how to approach the peasants in the course of practical work, how to organise the poor and middle peasants so as to be able at every step to combat their gravitation towards the past, their attempts to go back to free trading activities, their constant striving to be "free" producers. The word "freedom" is a good word. We meet it at every step: freedom to trade, freedom to sell, freedom to sell oneself, and so forth. And there are Mensheviks and Socialist-Revolutionaries, rascals, who garble and distort this beautiful word "freedom" in every newspaper and in every speech. But these are all crooks, capitalism's prostitutes, who are trying to drag the people back to the past.

Lastly, the main object of the attention and activities of the Council of People's Commissars as well as of the Council of Defence has recently, during the past few months and weeks, been the fight against the famine.

The famine is particularly disastrous for us at the present time, on the threshold of the spring; and the spring threatens to be a most severe period for us. Just as last year the most severe period was the end of winter, the spring and the beginning of the summer, so, this year, we are now on the threshold of a severe period. The white guards, landowners and capitalists have greater hopes of being able to play on the famine as a means of crushing Soviet power since they have been unable to do it in open struggle.

The people who call themselves Mensheviks and Right or Left Socialist-Revolutionaries have sunk so low that they claim to side with the working people but when the food situation becomes more acute and famine is approaching they try to take advantage of it and incite the masses of the people against the workers' and peasants' government. They do not understand that this sort of policy today, this incitement and these attempts by the Left Socialist-Revolutionaries to make capital out of the famine, ostensibly for the benefit of the workers, are direct assistance to the white guards, just as much as was the treachery of the Left Socialist-Revolutionary Muravyov on the Eastern Front last year, which cost the lives of tens of thousands of workers and peasants. Any such agitation costs thousands more lives in the war against the white guards. When Muravyov committed his act of treachery last year, he opened up almost the entire front to the enemy and caused us a number of severe reverses.

That is why I should like primarily and mainly to deal very briefly with the major facts.

Although today our food situation has become worse, just as it did last spring, we have every hope that we shall not only overcome this difficulty but shall cope with it better than we did last year. This hope is based on the fact that the situation in the East and South has greatly improved; and the East and South are the main granaries of Russia. At a number of meetings of the Council of Defence and the Council of People's Commissars held during the past few days we ascertained very definitely that about nine million poods of grain have been piled up on the railways between Kazan and Saratov, and on the Volga-Bugulma line, to the east of Samara, across the Volga.

The great difficulty, and great danger, is that our railways are in such a state of disrepair, and the shortage of locomotives is so considerable, that we are not sure of being able to move all this grain. This is what we have concentrated our main attention and activities on during the past few days, and that is why we resolved to resort to a measure like the suspension of all passenger traffic from March 18 to April 10.

We know that this is a harsh measure. Agitators who are helping the white guards will no doubt come along and shout, "Look, the people are starving, and yet passenger traffic has been stopped, to make it impossible to carry grain." Agitators of this type will certainly appear. But we tell ourselves that in all cases of difficulty we rely on the class-consciousness of the honest workers, and they will side with us.

According to the calculations of the experts, the suspension of passenger traffic will release 220 locomotives. These passenger locomotives are less powerful than freight locomotives, they cannot haul as much; but we have estimated that during this period they will be able to haul about three and a half million poods of grain. Individual food profiteers and the starving people who roam all over the country in search of grain, would, at the most, be able to carry half a million poods in such a period. This will be confirmed by every experienced railway worker, by everybody, who has been on the Trans-Volga line and has seen the grain heaped up, sometimes right on the bare snow. The sacks of grain may be damaged; as it is the grain is moist, and the situation will become worse when the spring thaw commences. We therefore resorted to this harsh measure, convinced that the truth cannot be concealed from the vast masses of the workers, that the Left Socialist-Revolutionaries will not succeed in misleading them, that truth will prevail.

This harsh measure, the suspension of passenger traffic, will provide us with several million poods of grain. We must brush aside the lies, slander and fairy-tales to the effect that it is harmful to suspend passenger traffic and say that with the assistance of the Petrograd, Moscow and Ivanovo-Voznesensk workers who are being sent to the South, it will provide a sufficient quantity of grain. Incidentally, I will remind you that no city has devoted so much effort to the organisation of food supplies as Petrograd. All the best forces in that city have already been mustered for the work, and this is what the workers in the other advanced cities should do, too.

The socialist revolution cannot be accomplished without the working class. It cannot be accomplished if the working class has not accumulated sufficient forces to be able to lead the tens of millions of exhausted, illiterate, and scattered rural people who had been crushed by capitalism. Only the advanced workers can lead them. But our best forces have already been used up, they are weary and exhausted. Their places must be taken by average people and young forces. Probably they will make mistakes, but that does not matter so long as they are devoted to the workers' cause, and so long as they have been brought up in the environment of the proletarian struggle.

We have already taken measures to send our best forces to the Volga-Bugulma Railway. Comrade Bryukhanov has gone there accompanied by a group of workers. Army detachments accompanied by workers have been sent to other lines, too, and, I repeat, there are good grounds for hoping that we shall obtain grain. A severe half-year lies ahead of us, but this will be the last severe half-year, because instead of an enemy who is becoming stronger, we have in front of us an enemy who is disintegrating, for the Soviet movement is growing in all countries.

These are the grounds on which, after discussing the matter most carefully and verifying our calculations again and again, we say that the suspension of passenger traffic will enable us to bring in several million poods of grain and use the extremely rich granaries of the East and South. In the course of this severe half-year we shall vanquish our chief enemy, the famine. Moreover, our position today is much better than it was last year, because we now have reserves.

Last year the Czechoslovaks reached Kazan and Simbirsk; the Ukraine was under the heel of the Germans; Krasnov, financed by the Germans, was mustering troops in the Don region, and we were cut off from the South. Today the Ukraine is being liberated from the German imperialists. The latter had planned to ship 60,000,000 poods of grain to Germany, but they shipped only 9,000,000 poods, and with it something they cannot digest, namely, Bolshevism. This is what upset the German imperialists, and this is what will upset the French and British imperialists if it becomes possible for them to advance farther into Russia.

We now have a Soviet Ukraine. And when it comes to supplying us with grain, the Soviet Government of the Ukraine will not fix its price like a huckster, a profiteer, or a muzhik who says, "The starving will give me a 1,000 rubles a pood. To hell with the state monopoly. All I want is to get rich. If the people are starving, all the better, they will pay more." This is the way the rural bourgeoisie, the kulaks, the profiteers argue, and they are being assisted by all those who agitate against the state grain monopoly, by those who stand for "freedom" to trade, that is, freedom for the rich muzhik to amass wealth, and freedom for the workers who are getting nothing to starve to death. But the Ukrainian Government said, "Our first task is to help the starving North. The Ukraine cannot hold out if the North, which is exhausted by famine, does not hold out. The Ukraine will hold out, and her victory will be certain, if she helps the starving North."

In the Ukraine there are huge stocks of grain. We cannot ship it all at once. We have sent our best Soviet forces to the Ukraine and already they all report in one voice that the stocks of grain are enormous, but they cannot be dispatched all at once, we haven't the machinery for it. The Germans devastated the Ukraine to such a degree that the machinery of administration must be built entirely anew, and this has only just begun. Complete chaos reigns there. The worst period, the first weeks at Smolny after the October Revolution when we were trying to overcome the chaos, was nothing compared with the difficulties that are now being experienced in the Ukraine. The Ukrainian comrades are complaining bitterly about the lack of people, lack of forces with which to build up the Soviet government. They have no machinery of administration, they have no proletarian centre like Petrograd or Moscow, for the Ukrainian proletarian centres are occupied by the enemy. Kiev is not a proletarian centre. The Donets Basin, exhausted by starvation, has not yet been liberated from the Cossacks. Our Ukrainian comrades cry, "Workers of the North, come to our assistance!"

And that is why we, on behalf of the Ukrainian comrades, say to the Petrograd workers, knowing that they have done more than the workers of any other city, "Do a little more, make another effort!" Now we can and must come to the aid of our Ukrainian comrades, because they must build up the machinery of the Soviet state on a site that was cleared and laid waste by suffering as no other place has been!

We discussed the situation in the Central Committee of our Party and gave instructions that everything should first be done to help to build up administrative machinery in the Ukraine, and in return for this, when this machinery is available, to set to work to obtain 50,000,000 poods of grain by June 1.

I do not in the least wish to assert that this will be done. We all know that of all the tasks we undertook, not one was fulfilled by the appointed date. Suppose only part of this task is fulfilled; at all events you will know definitely that when things get worse, when the famine here becomes more acute, and when the food supply machinery will be working at top speed in the East and South, we shall be able to obtain urgent aid from the South and improve our situation.

In addition to the Ukraine, we have another source of grain supply—the Don region. There, the victories of the Red Army have already worked miracles. Several weeks ago the situation on the Don, in the war against Krasnov, against our main enemy, against the officers and Cossacks who received millions in bribes, first from the Germans and then from the British and French, who are still continuing to help them—several weeks ago, our position was very serious. But now we have, with tremendous speed, regained territory not only up to Tsaritsyn, but farther to the south. The forces of Krasnov and the Don counter-revolutionaries have been broken in spite of the assistance they received from the imperialists.

What does this mean? It means that we are getting nearer to coal and grain, for the lack of which we are perishing—owing to the shortage of coal, the railways and factories are coming to a standstill, and owing to the shortage of grain, the workers in the towns, and in the non-agricultural districts generally, are suffering the pangs of starvation.

In the Don area, as in the Ukraine, the grain stocks are enormous. Furthermore, it cannot be said that there is no administrative machinery in the Don area. In every military unit there is a Communist group, worker commissars, and groups of food supply workers. The greatest difficulty there is that neither of the two main railway lines can be used because the white guards, on retreating, blew up the bridges.

The last meeting of the Council of Defence and the Council of People's Commissars was attended by experts whom we asked how material could be obtained to repair the lines, and how at least one of them could be repaired. At the last meeting of the Council of Defence we were able to assure ourselves that thanks to an enormous exertion of effort not only were materials provided, but the comrades on the spot assured us, almost guaranteed, that both lines would be repaired before the spring thaw. The resumption of traffic on these two lines is perhaps worth many victories over the Cossacks and enables us to say that we must hold on for another few severe months, we must strain every nerve, obtain the assistance of the Petrograd, Moscow and Ivanovo-Voznesensk workers. In addition to the East, from where it is difficult to ship anything, in addition to the Ukraine, where there are vast stocks but no administrative machinery, we have the Don region, which has been reconquered by the Red Army. That is why we cautiously, after cool calculation, after verifying all this by means of repeated reports and communications from the people on the spot and hearing the statements of food supply and railway experts, say that we have very good grounds for believing that we can not only hold out as we held out last year, but also greatly improve our conditions.

Our internal enemy is collapsing, and our external enemy cannot possibly hold out for long. Comrades, we were particularly convinced of this by what we heard from our foreign comrades who arrived here, and jointly with whom we recently formed the Communist International in Moscow. In Paris, speakers at public meetings who attack Bolshevism are driven from the platform. Yes, victory will be ours! The imperialists may yet shed the blood of thousands and thousands of workers, murder Rosa Luxemburg and Karl Liebknecht, and hundreds of the best representatives of the International, they may fill the prisons in Britain, France, Germany and Italy with socialists, but this will not avail them!

Victory will be ours! For in spite of all the lies and the torrents of abuse and filthy slander that are poured out against us, the workers of all countries now understand what is meant by Soviets, by Soviet power. The capitalists of no country have a way out. I repeat that when they conclude peace they will be at loggerheads. France is ready to hurl herself upon Italy, they are quarrelling over the division of the booty. Japan is arming against America. They have imposed upon the peoples an incredible burden of tribute, millions upon millions of war debts. But everywhere the people are exhausted by war, everywhere there is a shortage of food, industry is at a standstill, and starvation reigns. The Entente, which is promising right and left to help the counter-revolutionaries, cannot feed its own countries. The masses of the workers in Paris, in London and in New York have translated the word "Soviet" into their own languages, they have made it intelligible for every worker, for they know that the old bourgeois republic cannot help their cause, that only a workers' government can help them.

Soviet Russia encounters enormous difficulties because the military forces of the most well-armed and most powerful countries of the world have been hurled against her. In spite of this, Soviet power in Russia has succeeded in winning the sympathy, the attention and moral support of the workers of the world. And on the basis of these facts, not exaggerating in the least, and not shutting our eyes to the fact that in Germany and in other countries workers' blood is flowing and many of the best socialist leaders are being brutally done to death — we know this and do not shut our eyes to it — we assert that victory, complete victory, will be ours, because the power of the imperialists in the other countries has been shaken, while the workers are emerging from their state of stultification and deception. Soviet power has already won recognition from the workers of all countries. Everywhere the Soviets, the capture of power by the workers themselves, are regarded as the only hope.

And when the workers learn that the united workers even in an underdeveloped and backward country, after capturing power, have succeeded in creating a force that is resisting the imperialists of the whole world, when they learn that these workers have succeeded in taking the factories from the capitalists and in giving to the peasants the land that formerly belonged to the landowners—when this truth reaches the masses of workers of all countries, we shall be able once again to say loudly, and with firm conviction, that our victory on a world scale is assured, for the power of the bourgeoisie has been shaken, it will no longer succeed in deceiving the workers, for the Soviet movement has sprung up everywhere. And iust as we saw the birth of the Soviet Republic on October 25, 1917, and the birth of the Third, Communist International a few days ago in Moscow, so we shall soon see the birth of a World Soviet Republic. (The speech was interrupted by applause and ended in an ovation.)

I should very much like the Petrograd comrades to print the following as a foreword or afterword to my speech, even if only in small type.

April 17

Speech At A Plenary Session Of The Moscow Soviet

November 20, 1922
Lenin Collected Works, Volume 33, pages 435-443

Comrades, I regret very much and apologise that I have been unable to come to your session earlier. As far as I know you intended a few weeks ago to give me an opportunity of attending the Moscow Soviet. I could not come because after my illness, from December onwards, I was incapacitated, to use the professional term, for quite a long time, and because of this reduced ability to work had to postpone my present address from week to week. A very considerable portion of my work which, as you will remember, I had first piled on Comrade Tsyurupa, and then on Comrade Rykov, I also had to pile additionally on Comrade Kamenev. And I must say that, to employ a simile I have already used, he was suddenly burdened with two loads. Though, to continue the simile, it should be said that the horse has proved to be an exceptionally capable and zealous one. (Applause.) All the same, however, nobody is supposed to drag two loads, and I am now waiting impatiently for Comrades Tsyurupa and Rykov to return, and we shall divide up the work at least a little more fairly. As for myself, in view of my reduced ability to work it takes me much more time to look into matters than I should like.

In December 1921, when I had to stop working altogether, it was the year's end. We were effecting the transition to the New Economic Policy, and it turned out already then that, although we had embarked upon this transition in the beginning of 1921, it was quite a difficult, I would say a very difficult, transition. We have now been effecting this transition for more than eighteen months, and one would think that it was time the majority took up new places and disposed themselves according to the new conditions, particularly those of the New Economic Policy.

As to foreign policy, we had the fewest changes in that field. We pursued the line that we had adopted earlier, and I think I can say with a clear conscience that we pursued it quite consistently and with enormous success. There is no need, I think, to deal with that in detail; the capture of Vladivostok, the ensuing demonstration and the declaration of federation which you read in the press the other day have proved and shown with the utmost clarity that no changes are necessary in this respect. The road we are on is absolutely clearly and well defined and has ensured us success in face of all the countries of the world, although some of them are still prepared to declare that they refuse to sit at one table with us. Nevertheless, economic relations, followed by diplomatic relations, are improving, must improve, and certainly will improve. Every country which resists this risks being late, and, perhaps in some quite substantial things, it risks being at a disadvantage. All of us see this now, and not only from the press, from the newspapers. I think that in their trips abroad comrades are also finding the changes very great. In that respect, to use an old simile, we have not changed to other trains, or to other conveyances.

But as regards our home policy, the change we made in the spring of 1921, which was necessitated by such extremely powerful and convincing circumstances that no debates or disagreements arose among us about it—that change continues to cause us some difficulties, great difficulties, I would say. Not because we have any doubts about the need for the turn—no doubts exist in that respect—not because we have any doubts as to whether the test of our New Economic Policy has yielded the successes we expected. No doubts exist on that score—I can say this quite definitely— either in the ranks of our Party or in the ranks of the huge mass of non-Party workers and peasants.

In this sense the problem presents no difficulties. The difficulties we have stem from our being faced with a task whose solution very often requires the services of new people, extraordinary measures and extraordinary methods. Doubts still exist among us as to whether this or that is correct. There are changes in one direction or another. And it should be said that both will continue for quite a long time. "The New Economic Policy!" A strange title. It was called a New Economic Policy because it turned things back. We are now retreating, going back, as it were; but we are doing so in order, after first retreating, to take a running start and make a bigger leap forward. It was on this condition alone that we retreated in pursuing our New Economic Policy. Where and how we must now regroup, adapt and reorganise in order to start a most stubborn offensive after our retreat, we do not yet know. To carry out all these operations properly we need, as the proverb says, to look not ten but a hundred times before we leap. We must do so in order to cope with the incredible difficulties we encounter in dealing with all our tasks and problems. You know perfectly well what sacrifices have been made to achieve what has been achieved; you know how long the Civil War has dragged on and what effort it has cost. Well now, the capture of Vladivostok has shown all of us (though Vladivostok is a long way off, it is after all one of our own towns) (prolonged applause) everybody's desire to join us, to join in our achievements. The Russian Soviet Federative Socialist Republic now stretches from here to there. This desire has rid us both of our civil enemies and of the foreign enemies who attacked us. I am referring to Japan.

We have won quite a definite diplomatic position, recognised by the whole world. All of you see it. You see its results, but how much time we needed to get it! We have now won the recognition of our rights by our enemies both in economic and in commercial policy. This is proved by the conclusion of trade agreements.

We can see why we, who eighteen months ago took the path of the so-called New Economic Policy, are finding it so incredibly difficult to advance along that path. We live in a country devastated so severely by war, knocked out of anything like the normal course of life, in a country that has suffered and endured so much, that willy-nilly we are beginning all our calculations with a very, very small percentage—the pre-war percentage. We apply this yardstick to the conditions of our life, we sometimes do so very impatiently, heatedly, and always end up with the conviction that the difficulties are vast. The task we have set ourselves in this field seems all the more vast because we are comparing it with the state of affairs in any ordinary bourgeois country. We have set ourselves this task because we understood that it was no use expecting the wealthy powers to give us the assistance usually forthcoming under such circumstances.[3] After the Civil War we have been subjected to very nearly a boycott, that is, we have been told that the economic ties that are customary and normal in the capitalist world will not be maintained in our case.

Over eighteen months have passed since we undertook the New Economic Policy, and even a longer period has passed since we concluded our first international treaty. Nonetheless, this boycott of us by all the bourgeoisie and all governments continues to be felt. We could not count on anything else when we adopted the new economic conditions; yet we had no doubt that we had to make the change and achieve success single-handed. The further we go, the clearer it becomes that any aid that may be rendered to us, that will be rendered to us by the capitalist powers, will, far from eliminating this condition, in all likelihood and in the overwhelming majority of cases intensify it, accentuate it still further. "Single-handed" — we told ourselves. "Single-handed" — we are told by almost every capitalist country with which we have concluded any deals, with which we have undertaken any engagements, with which we have begun any negotiations. And that is where the special difficulty lies. We must realise this difficulty. We have built up our own political system in more than three years of work, incredibly hard work that was incredibly full of heroism. In the position in which we were till now we had no time to see whether we would smash something needlessly, no time to see whether there would be many sacrifices, because there were sacrifices enough, because the struggle which we then began (you know this perfectly well and there is no need to dwell on it) was a life-and-death struggle against the old social system, against which we fought to forge for ourselves a right to existence, to peaceful development. And we have won it. It is not we who say this, it is not the testimony of witnesses who may be accused of being partial to us. It is the testimony of witnesses who are in the

145

camp of our enemies and who are naturally partial—not in our favour, however, but against us. These witnesses were in Denikin's camp. They directed the occupation. And we know that their partiality cost us very dear, cost us colossal destruction. We suffered all sorts of losses on their account, and lost values of all kinds, including the greatest of all values—human lives—on an incredibly large scale. Now we must scrutinise our tasks most carefully and understand that the main task will be not to give up our previous gains. We shall not give up a single one of our old gains. (Applause.) Yet we are also faced with an entirely new task; the old may prove a downright obstacle. To understand this task is most difficult. Yet it must be understood, so that we may learn how to work when, so to speak, it is necessary to turn ourselves inside out. I think, comrades, that these words and slogans are understandable, because for nearly a year, during my enforced absence, you have had in practice, handling the jobs on hand, to speak and think of this in various ways and on hundreds of occasions, and I am confident that your reflections on that score can only lead to one conclusion, namely, that today we must display still more of the flexibility which we employed till now in the Civil War.

We must not abandon the old. The series of concessions that adapt us to the capitalist powers is a series of concessions that enables them to make contact with us, ensures them a profit which is sometimes bigger, perhaps, than it should be. At the same time, we are conceding but a little part of the means of production, which are held almost entirely by our state. The other day the papers discussed the concession proposed by the Englishman Urquhart, who has hitherto been against us almost throughout the Civil War. He used to say: "We shall achieve our aim in the Civil War against Russia, against the Russia that has dared to deprive us of this and of that." And after all that we had to enter into negotiations with him. We did not refuse them, we undertook them with the greatest joy, but we said: "Beg your pardon, but we shall not give up what we have won. Our Russia is so big, our economic potentialities are so numerous, and we feel justified in not rejecting your kind proposal, but we shall discuss it soberly, like businessmen." True, nothing came of our first talk, because we could not agree to his proposal for political reasons. We had to reject it. So long as the British did not entertain the possibility of our participating in the negotiations on the Straits, the Dardanelles, we had to reject it, but right after doing so we had to start examining the matter in substance. We discussed whether or not it was of advantage to us, whether we would profit from concluding this concession agreement, and if so, under what circumstances it would be profitable. We had to talk about the price. That, comrades, is what shows you clearly how much our present approach to problems should differ from our former approach. Formerly the Communist said: "I give my life", and it seemed very simple to him, although it was not always so simple. Now, however, we Communists face quite another task. We must now take all things into account, and each of you must learn to be prudent. We must calculate how, in the capitalist environment, we can ensure our existence, how we can profit by our enemies, who, of course, will bargain, who have never forgotten how to bargain and will bargain at our expense. We are not forgetting that either, and do not in the least imagine commercial people anywhere turning into lambs and, having turned into lambs, offering us blessings of all sorts for nothing. That does not happen, and we do not expect it, but count on the fact that we, who are accustomed to putting up a fight, will find a way out and prove capable of trading, and profiting, and emerging safely from difficult economic situations. That is a very difficult task. That is the task we are working on now. I should like us to realise clearly how great is the abyss between the old and the new tasks. However great the abyss may be, we learned to manoeuvre during the war, and we must understand that the manoeuvre we now have to perform, in the midst of which we now are, is the most difficult one. But then it seems to be our last manoeuvre. We must test our strength in this field and prove that we have learned more than just the lessons of yesterday and do not just keep repeating the fundamentals. Nothing of the kind. We have begun to relearn and shall relearn in such a way that we shall achieve definite and obvious success. And it is for the sake of this relearning, I think, that we must again firmly promise one another that under the name of the New Economic Policy we have turned back, but turned back in such a way as to surrender nothing of the new, and yet to give the capitalists such advantages as will compel any state, however hostile to us, to establish contacts and to deal with us. Comrade Krasin, who has had many talks with Urquhart, the head and backbone of the whole intervention, said that Urquhart, after all his attempts to foist the old system on us at all costs, throughout Russia, seated himself at the same table with him, with Krasin, and began asking: "What's the price? How much? For how many years?" (Applause.) This is still quite far from our concluding concession deals and thus entering into treaty relations that are perfectly precise and binding—from the viewpoint of bourgeois society—but we can already see that we are coming to it, have nearly come to it, but have not quite arrived. We must admit that, comrades, and not be swell-headed. We are still far from having fully achieved the things that will make us strong, self-reliant, and calmly confident that no capitalist deals can frighten us, calmly confident that however difficult a deal may be we shall conclude it, we shall get to the bottom of it and settle it. That is why the work— both political and Party—that we have begun in this sphere must be continued, and that is why we must change from the old methods to entirely new ones.

We still have the old machinery, and our task now is to remold it along new lines. We cannot do so at once, but we must see to it that the Communists we have are properly placed. What we need is that they, the Communists, should control the machinery they are assigned to, and not, as so often happens with us, that the machinery should control them. We should make no secret of it, and speak of it, frankly. Such are the tasks and the difficulties that confront us—and that at a moment when we have set out on our practical path, when we must not approach socialism as if it were an icon painted in festive colours. We need to take the right direction, we need to see that everything is checked, that the masses, the entire population, check the path we follow and say: "Yes, this is better than the old system." That is the task we have set ourselves. Our Party, a little group of people in comparison with the country's total population, has tackled this job. This tiny nucleus has set itself the task of remaking everything, and it will do so. We have proved that this is no utopia but a cause which people live by. We have all seen this. This has already been done. We must remake things in such a way that the great majority of the masses, the peasants and workers, will say: "It is not you who praise yourselves, but we. We say that you have achieved splendid results, after which no intelligent person will ever dream of returning to the old." We have not reached that point yet. That is why NEP remains the main, current, and all embracing slogan of today.We shall not forget a single one of the slogans we learned yesterday. We can say that quite calmly, without the slightest hesitation, say it to anybody, and every step we take demonstrates it. But we still have to adapt ourselves to the New Economic Policy. We must know how to overcome, to reduce to a definite minimum all its negative features, which there is no need to enumerate and which you know perfectly well. We must know how to arrange everything shrewdly. Our legislation gives us every opportunity to do so. Shall we be able to get things going properly? That is still-far from being settled. We are making a study of things. Every issue of our Party newspaper offers you a dozen articles which tell you that at such-and-such a factory, owned by so-and-so, the rental terms are such-and-such, whereas at another, where our Communist comrade is the manager, the terms are such-and-such. Does it yield a profit or not, does it pay its way or not? We have approached the very core of the everyday problems, and that is a tremendous achievement. Socialism is no longer a matter of the distant future, or an abstract picture, or an icon. Our opinion of icons is the same— a very bad one. **We have brought socialism into everyday life and must here see how matters stand. That is the task of our day**, the task of our epoch. Permit me to conclude by expressing confidence that difficult as this task may be, new as it may be compared with our previous task, and numerous as the difficulties may be that it entails, we shall all—not in a day, but in a few years—all of us together fulfil it whatever the cost, so that NEP **Russia will become socialist Russia.** (Stormy, prolonged applause.)

On the Final Victory of Socialism in the U.S.S.R.

18 January 1938 - 12 February 1938
J. V. Stalin
Ivan Philipovich Ivanov, staff propagandist of the Manturovsk District of the Young Communist League in the Kursk Region of the U.S.S.R., addressed a letter to Comrade Stalin requesting his opinion on the question of the final victory of Socialism in the Soviet Union.

IVANOV TO STALIN

Dear Comrade Stalin,

I earnestly request you to explain the following question : In the local districts here and even in the Regional Committee of the Young Communist League, a two-fold conception prevails about the final victory of socialism in our country, i.e., the first group of contradictions is confused with the second.

In your works on the destiny of Socialism in the U.S.S.R. you speak of two groups of contradictions - internal and external.

As for the first group of contradictions, we have, of course, solved them - within the country Socialism is victorious.

I would like to have your answer about the second group of contradictions, i.e., those between the land of Socialism and capitalism.

You point out that the final victory of Socialism implies the solution of the external contradictions, that we must be fully guaranteed against intervention and, consequently, against the restoration of capitalism.

But this group of contradictions can only be solved by the efforts of the workers of all countries.

Besides, Comrade Lenin taught us that "we can achieve final victory only on a world scale, only by the joint efforts of the workers of all countries."

While attending the class for staff propagandists at the Regional Committee of the Y.C.L., I, basing myself on your works, said that the final victory of Socialism is possible only on a world scale. But the leading regional committee workers - Urozhenko, First Secretary of the Regional Committee, and Kazelkov, propaganda instructor - described my statement as a Trotskyist sortie.

I began to read to them passages from your works on this question, but Urozhenko ordered me to close the book and said : "Comrade Stalin said this in 1926, but we are now in 1938. At that time we did not have the final victory, but now we have it and there is no need for us at all to worry about intervention and restoration."

Then he went on to say : "We have now the final victory of Socialism and a full guarantee against intervention and the restoration of capitalism."

And so I was counted as an abettor of Trotskyism and removed from propaganda work and the question was raised as to whether I was fit to remain in the Y.C.L.

Please, Comrade Stalin, will you explain whether we have the final victory of Socialism yet or not, Perhaps there is additional contemporary material on this question connected with recent changes that I have not come across yet. Also I think that Urozhenko's statement that Comrade Stalin's works on this question are somewhat out of date is an anti-Bolshevik one.

Are the leading workers of the Regional Committee right in counting me as a Trotskyist? I feel very much hurt and offended over this.

I hope, Comrade Stalin, that you will grant my request and reply to the Manturovsk District, Kursk Region, First Zasemsky Village Soviet, Ivan Philipovich Ivanov.

(Signed) I. Ivanov.

January 18, 1938.

STALIN TO IVANOV

Of course you are right, Comrade Ivanov, and your ideological opponents, i.e., Comrades Urozhenko and Kazelkov, are wrong. And for the following reasons :

Undoubtedly the question of the victory of Socialism in one country, in this case our country, has two different sides.

The first side of the question of the victory of Socialism in our country embraces the problem of the mutual relations between classes in our country. This concerns the sphere of internal relations.

Can the working class of our country overcome the contradictions with our peasantry and establish an alliance, collaboration with them?

Can the working class of our country, in alliance - with our peasantry, smash the bourgeoisie of our country, deprive it of the land, factories, mines, etc., and by its own efforts build a new, classless society, complete Socialist society?

Such are the problems that are connected with the first side of the question of the victory of Socialism in our country.

Leninism answers these problems in the affirmative.

Lenin teaches us that "we have all that is necessary for the building of a complete Socialist society."

Hence, we can and must, by our own efforts, overcome our bourgeoisie and build Socialist society.

Trotsky, Zinoviev, Kamenev, and those other gentlemen who later became spies and agents of fascism, denied that it was possible to build Socialism in our country unless the victory of the Socialist revolution was first achieved in other countries, in capitalist countries. As a matter of fact, these gentlemen wanted to turn our country back to the path of bourgeois development and they concealed their apostasy by hypocritically talking about the "victory of the revolution" in other countries.

This was precisely the point of controversy between our Party and these gentlemen.

Our country's subsequent course of development proved that the Party was right, and that Trotsky and company were wrong.

For, during this period, we succeeded in liquidating our bourgeoisie, in establishing fraternal collaboration with our peasantry and in building, in the main, Socialist society, notwithstanding the fact that the Socialist revolution has not yet been victorious in other countries.

This is the position in regard to the first side of the question of the victory of Socialism in our country.

I think, Comrade Ivanov, that this is not the side of the question that is the point of controversy between you and Comrades Urozhenko and Kazelkov.

The second side of the question of the victory of Socialism in our country embraces the problem of the mutual relations between our country and other countries, capitalist countries; the problem of the mutual relations between the working class of our country and the bourgeoisie of other countries. This concerns the sphere of external, international relations.

Can the victorious Socialism of one country, which is encircled by many strong capitalist countries, regard itself as being fully guaranteed against the danger of military invasion, and hence, against attempts to restore capitalism in our country?

Can our working class and our peasantry, by their own efforts, without the serious assistance of the working class in capitalist countries, overcome the bourgeoisie of other countries in the same way as we overcame our own bourgeoisie? In other words :

Can we regard the victory of Socialism in our country as final, i.e., as being free from the dangers of military attack and of attempts to restore capitalism, assuming that Socialism is victorious only in one country and that the capitalist encirclement continues to exist?

Such are the problems that are connected with the second side of the question of the victory of Socialism in our country.

Leninism answers these problems in the negative.

Leninism teaches that "the final victory of Socialism, in the sense of full guarantee against the restoration of bourgeois relations, is possible only on an international scale" (c.f. resolution of the Fourteenth Conference of the Communist Party of the Soviet Union).

This means that the serious assistance of the international proletariat is a force without which the problem of the final victory of Socialism in one country cannot be solved.

This, of course, does not mean that we must sit with folded arms and wait for assistance from outside.

On the contrary, this assistance of the international proletariat must be combined with our work to strengthen the defence of our country, to strengthen the Red Army and the Red Navy, to mobilise the whole country for the purpose of resisting military attack and attempts to restore bourgeois relations.

This is what Lenin says on this score :

"We are living not merely in a State but in a system of States, and it is inconceivable that the Soviet Republic should continue to coexist for a long period side by side with imperialist States. Ultimately one or other must conquer. Meanwhile, a number of terrible clashes between the Soviet Republic and the bourgeois States is inevitable. This means that if the proletariat, as the ruling class, wants to and will rule, it must prove this also by military organization." (Collected Works, Vol. 24. P. 122.)

And further :

"We are surrounded by people, classes and governments which openly express their hatred for us. We must remember that we are at all times but a hair's breadth from invasion." (Collected Works, Vol. 27. P. 117.)

This is said sharply and strongly but honestly and truthfully without embellishment as Lenin was able to speak.

On the basis of these premises Stalin stated in "Problems of Leninism" that:

"The final victory of Socialism is the full guarantee against attempts at intervention, and that means against restoration, for any serious attempt at restoration can take place only with serious support from outside, only with the support of international capital.

"Hence the support of our revolution by the workers of all countries, and still more, the victory of the workers in at least several countries, is a necessary condition for fully guaranteeing the first victorious country against attempts at intervention and restoration, a necessary condition for the final victory of Socialism," (Problems of Leninism, 1937. P. 134.)

Indeed, it would be ridiculous and stupid to close our eyes to the capitalist encirclement and to think that our external enemies, the fascists, for example, will not, if the opportunity arises, make an attempt at a military attack upon the U.S.S.R. Only blind braggarts or masked enemies who desire to lull the vigilance of our people can think like that.

No less ridiculous would it be to deny that in the event of the slightest success of military intervention, the interventionists would try to destroy the Soviet system in the districts they occupied and restore the bourgeois system.

Did not Denikin and Kolchak restore the bourgeois system in the districts they occupied? Are the fascists any better than Denikin or Kolchak?

Only blockheads or masked enemies who with their boastfulness want to conceal their hostility and are striving to demobilise the people, can deny the danger of military intervention and attempts at restoration as long as the capitalist encirclement exists.

Can the victory of Socialism in one country be regarded as final if this country is encircled by capitalism, and if it is not fully guaranteed against the danger of intervention and restoration?

Clearly, it cannot, This is the position in regard to the question of the victory of Socialism in one country.

It follows that this question contains two different problems :

1. The problem of the internal relations in our country, i.e., the problem of overcoming our own bourgeoisie and building complete Socialism; and

2. The problem of the external relations of our country, i.e., the problem of completely ensuring our country against the dangers of military intervention and restoration.

We have already solved the first problem, for our bourgeoisie has already been liquidated and Socialism has already been built in the main. This is what we call the victory of Socialism, or, to be more exact, the victory of Socialist Construction in one country.

We could say that this victory is final if our country were situated on an island and if it were not surrounded by numerous capitalist countries.

But as we are not living on an island but "in a system of States," a considerable number of which are hostile to the land of Socialism and create the danger of intervention and restoration, we say openly and honestly that the victory of Socialism in our country is not yet final.

But from this it follows that the second problem is not yet solved and that it has yet to be solved.

More than that : the second problem cannot be solved in the way that we solved the first problem, i.e., solely by the efforts of our country.

The second problem can be solved only by combining the serious efforts of the international proletariat with the still more serious efforts of the whole of our Soviet people.

The international proletarian ties between the working class of the U.S.S.R. and the working class in bourgeois countries must be increased and strengthened; the political assistance of the working class in the bourgeois countries for the working class of our country must be organized in the event of a military attack on our country; and also every assistance of the working class of our country for the working class in bourgeois countries must be organized; our Red Army, Red Navy, Red Air Fleet, and the Chemical and Air Defence Society must be increased and strengthened to the utmost.

The whole of our people must be kept in a state of mobilisation and preparedness in the face of the danger of a military attack, so that no "accident" and no tricks on the part of our external enemies may take us by surprise . . .

From your letter it is evident that Comrade Urozhenko adheres to different and not quite Leninist opinions. He, it appears, asserts that "we now have the final victory of Socialism and full guarantee against intervention and the restoration of capitalism."

There cannot be the slightest doubt that Comrade Urozhenko is fundamentally wrong.

Comrade Urozhenko's assertion can be explained only by his failure to understand the surrounding reality and his ignorance of the elementary propositions of Leninism, or by empty boastfulness of a conceited young bureaucrat.

If it is true that "we have full guarantee against intervention and restoration of capitalism," then why do we need a strong Red Army, Red Navy, Red Air Fleet, a strong Chemical and Air Defence Society, more and stronger ties with the international proletariat?

Would it not be better to spend the milliards that now go for the purpose of strengthening the Red Army on other needs and to reduce the Red Army to the utmost, or even to dissolve it altogether?

People like Comrade Urozhenko, even if subjectively they are loyal to our cause, are objectively dangerous to it because by their boastfulness they - willingly or unwillingly (it makes no difference!) - lull the vigilance of our people, demobilise the workers and peasants and help the enemies to take us by surprise in the event of international complications.

As for the fact that, as it appears, you, Comrade Ivanov, have been "removed from propaganda work and the question has been raised of your fitness to remain in the Y.C.L.," you have nothing to fear.

If the people in the Regional Committee of the Y.C.L. really want to imitate Chekov's Sergeant Prishibeyev, you can be quite sure that they will lose on this game.

Prishibeyevs are not liked in our country.

Now you can judge whether the passage from the book "Problems of Leninism" on the victory of Socialism in one country is out of date or not.

I myself would very much like it to be out of date.

I would like unpleasant things like capitalist encirclement, the danger of military attack, the danger of the restoration of capitalism, etc., to be things of the past. Unfortunately, however, these unpleasant things still exist.

(Signed) J. Stalin.

February 12, 1938.

Pravda, 14 February 1938